To: Alan
Ride 'em
Fred

FREDERIC REMINGTON
THE AMERICAN WEST

This edition is published by Bonanza Books,
distributed by Crown Publishers, Inc.
by arrangement with Volair Limited.

h g f e d c b a

1981 EDITION

Manufactured in the United States of America

Library of Congress Cataloging in Publication Data
Main entry under title:

Frederic Remington, the American West.

Bibliography: p. 325
Includes index.
1. Remington, Frederic, 1861-1909.
2. West (U.S.) in art.   I. Remington,
Frederic, 1861-1909.   II. St. Clair, Philip R.
III. American Museum of Natural History.
IV. Title: The American West.
NC975.5.R45A4 1982   741.973   81-18077
ISBN 0-517-361825   AACR2

FREDERIC REMINGTON
THE AMERICAN WEST

An Official Publication of the
American Museum of Natural History

Selected and Edited
by
Philip R. St. Clair

Bonanza • New York

FREDERIC REMINGTON 1861–1909

Photograph courtesy of the Remington Art Museum,
Ogdensburg, New York.

TABLE OF CONTENTS

INTRODUCTION

"The cavalryman, the Indian, the scout, the miner, and the ranchman have furnished Frederic Remington with subjects that he illustrates with much vigor of line and striking effect. His drawing of horses in motion is spirited, and even if it is exaggerated sometimes, there is always a general look of truth and life and dash. In his pictures of life on the plains, and of Indian fighting, he has almost created a new field of illustration, so fresh and novel are his characterizations; and the hot, sandy plains, with soldiers marching doggedly under the burning sun, the vast prairies with the cowboys in lonely watch over their herds, the frontier towns with their motley population of whites and half-breeds, are realized as they have never been before."

Written by William A. Coffin in an article for *Scribner's Magazine* in March, 1892, these accolades were accorded a man who, at age thirty-one, had made an indelible and profound mark on the world of illustration. Yet as young as it was, Frederic Remington's career as an artist had taken a fascinating and circuitous route.

Seth Pierpont Remington founded the *St. Lawrence Plaindealer* in Canton, a small town in upper New York State. Several years later, on October 4, 1861, a son was born to Clara Sackrider Remington and Seth, whom they named Frederic Sackrider. A year later, Seth left his livelihood as a staunch Republican journalist to become a recruiter for a Union cavalry regiment. Although his highest rank was Major, the community dubbed him "colonel" when he came home to his wife, friends, and a five-year-old son who loved hearing of his father's exploits.

The Remingtons lived in Bloomington, Illinois for about a year after Seth's retirement from military service, then returned to Canton where the Colonel repurchased the *St. Lawrence Plaindealer*. Young Fred relished his father's new avocation—horse and harness racing. With Walter Van Valkenberg, Seth had formed a partnership; Valkenberg trained and rode, while the Colonel subsidized the enterprise. Fred trailed the partners, becoming a student of horse conformation and an adept at riding, handling a buggy and driving racing sulkies. Fred's penchant for horses eventually grew from infatuation to devoted affection. "I hardly need to say that he loves the horse," his friend Julian Ralph later wrote, "but what not everyone knows is that he has said he would be proud to have carved on his tombstone the simple sentence, 'He knew the horse'. . . ."[1]

In 1870, President Grant appointed Seth to the position of U.S. Collector of the Port of Ogdensburg, New York. The appointment was timely, for in the two previous years fires had destroyed the two Canton print shops he had owned. The Colonel was rewarded for his continued devotion to the cause of the Republican party. Again the *Plaindealer* was sold, but journalistic and political zeal soon led the Colonel again into editorship, this time for the *Ogdensburg Journal*.

At age fourteen Fred was sent to the Vermont Episcopal Institute in Burlington. From hearing his father's war stories, he had become fascinated with things military: in a letter home to his boyhood friend John Howard, he wrote, "I got out of drilling this afternoon of a sore foot in order to see the drill; a fellow can't see nothing while in ranks."[2] His schooling was continued in 1876 at the Highland Military Academy in Worchester, Massachusetts, where he remained for the next two years. "As a student of books he was undoubtedly lazy, but he had not a drop of slowly moving blood when it came to carrying a musket on the parade ground. . . . Also, he had developed a passion for drawing pictures. He had not received any instruction in art, but his sketches were marked by originality and freedom from copying."[3]

In the fall of 1878 Fred enrolled in the School of Fine Arts at Yale. The three-year program included drawing, perspective, anatomy, compositions and lectures.[4] Not three months after his arrival, a cartoon by Remington appeared in *The Yale Courant*. Titled "College Riff-Raff," the sketch depicted a heavily-bandaged football player, seated with plastered foot resting on a chair. A visitor has entered the room and asks, " 'Good gracious, old fellow, what have you been doing with yourself?' Rusher on the University football team: 'Oh! nothing in particular; a fellow must get used to the Rugby rules, you know. The doctor says I'll be all right by Thanksgiving, and that's all I care for now.' "[5] It was a spirited though innocently autobiographical introduction into the spectrum of illustration. As in art, Remington's interest in football was not passive. He played on the Yale team and also participated in boxing and horsemanship.

Remington found that his training in art was not equal to the athletics program or his taste for spontaneous drawing. According to Poultney Bigelow, a classmate and friend of Remington's at Yale, their mentors took not "the slightest interest in our efforts to draw."[6] Remington's gradual dissatisfaction with higher education was culminated by a tragic event on February 18, 1879 — his father's death. Coupled with his scholastic ennui were financial problems and the antipathy of his new guardian, Lamartin Z. Remington, toward art. Uncle Mart was "vehemently . . . opposed to having any men artists in the family and . . . desired to have him carry on the family tradition of writer-politician. . . ."[7] Convinced not to return to Yale, Remington moved to Uncle Mart's home in Albany and found employment as an executive clerk in the Governor's office in March of 1880. Two more clerical positions followed. All three proved equally boring.

Remington "was counted a good fellow but a poor clerk."[8] Sketches of fellow employees received more attention than desk work. At any excuse he would arrange a boxing bout or a horse racing adventure. "On one occasion Remington and a fellow clerk, John Holmes, were cutting 'cross country near Hurst's when Remington whipped out his revolver, discharged it and screeched to such an extent that both horses ran away."[9]

This scene, more akin to a cowboy saga than a rural New York steeplechase, presaged Remington's first venture into the American West. The clerical business was not fulfilling, and his dream of marrying Eva Caten, the beauty of Gloversville, New York, went unfulfilled. Her father had denied consent, perhaps due to the clerk's dim future. Remington thus planned a two-month escape from the dull environment. "At nineteen, I caught the fever to go west," Remington later told an interviewer, "and incidentally to become rich. That was my idea; art came second."[10]

The riches Remington desired eluded him, yet he returned to Albany with a gold mine in his portfolio — numerous sketches drawn on his travels. Remington set up an appointment with George William Curtis of *Harper's Weekly*, and the interview proved successful. Curtis bought one of his drawings, and it soon appeared as a full-page illustration.

COW-BOYS OF ARIZONA—ROUSED BY A SCOUT.—Drawn by W. A. Rogers, from a Sketch by Frederic Remington.

Remington's first trip west determined his future. No longer would an office job suffice. On October 4, 1882 Remington was twenty-one, had control of his inheritance, and by late the following February had decided to seek his fortune in Kansas. A Yale crony, Robert Camp, had written from eastern Kansas, glorifying the outdoor life, self-employment and sheep ranching. Remington joined his friend to observe the operation and thereafter bought a quarter section near Peabody. Although the ranch soon doubled in size, Remington sold the place in a year and moved to Kansas City. The experience was not wasted, however, as "a new epoch in his life began when he buckled a cartridge belt around his waist and put an ivory-handled Colt on his hip. . . . The ranch was a stirring place, the Indians were a reality and the cowboy was a picturesque being; the mustang had not been supplanted by the mule and the coyote skulked around every 'stake-out.'" [11]

On October 2, 1884 the Gloversville *Intelligencer* announced "the marriage of Mr. Frederic Remington of Kansas City, Mo., to Miss Eva Caten of this village. . . . The happy couple left on the two o'clock train for their future home in Kansas City, Mo., followed by the best wishes of many friends." Once again Remington invested in a Kansan enterprise—this time, a saloon. A *Kansas City Star* reporter recalled that Remington, " . . . along in the boom days of the '80s, was one of the gayest sports of Kansas City. His pursuit was of a good time and he wanted everyone to know it. He wore clothes and affected a demeanor further to advertise his hilarity of purpose. But when he realized that a saloon investment had been unprofitable, and that he was on the verge of being penniless, there came a most wonderful rebound in the man's mind. The listless intellect suddenly was lightened to receptivity; he set to work with a vigor that was natural in him; he painted. . . ." [12]

Missie, as Remington called his wife, returned east to Gloversville, freeing her husband to travel in the West. The Houghs of Kansas City befriended the starving artist and later recalled that "he was a young giant in those days, full of exuberance and carrying a portfolio of sketches." [13] Remington had sold a second illustration to Harper's Weekly. Although the sketch was crudely done, Henry Harper was pleased with its "ring of new and live material." [14]

The Houghs subsidized Remington's return east. He admitted later that "I tried 'rousting about' in the West but when I struck hard-pan I found that I was rubbing vs. natural laws and so I came East and entered Art." [15] Remington rejoined Missie, and they moved to Brooklyn. After vain attempts to sell his work to various magazines, he enrolled in the Art Students League in New York City in March of 1886. Consistent with his intolerance for the academic milieu, Remington stayed only three months—long enough, however, to learn techniques for refining his skills.

That summer Remington traveled beyond the Mississippi, this time into the Southwest. Thwarted in his desire to locate Geronimo, the artist nonetheless returned overwhelmed by the cadence of military life and the scenery of Colorado, New Mexico, Arizona and northern Mexico. "In all the world there is no such cheerless place, and the Indian for unknown generations has been reared and tarried in this peculiar land." [16] This trip, more than any other of his forays into the West, established Remington's future, for it was soon thereafter that he aggressively sought publishers for his impressions and that his success as an illustrator was sealed.

In November of 1886, *St. Nicholas* reproduced two of his drawings, and in December, *Outing* featured several of his sketches. The editor of *Outing*, Poultney Bigelow, had been a friend of Remington's at Yale. When the artist wandered into the editor's offices, the meeting proved a grand reunion, highlighted by Bigelow's purchase of Remington's entire portfolio.

HARPER'S WEEKLY.

JOURNAL OF CIVILIZATION.

VOL. XXX.—No. 1516.
Copyright, 1886, by HARPER & BROTHERS.

NEW YORK, SATURDAY, JANUARY 9, 1886.

TEN CENTS A COPY.
$4.00 PER YEAR, IN ADVANCE.

THE APACHE WAR—INDIAN SCOUTS ON GERONIMO'S TRAIL.—DRAWN BY FREDERIC REMINGTON.—[SEE PAGE 26.]

In subsequent years a number of editors took credit for giving Remington his start, including Bigelow. In his book *Seventy Summers*, Bigelow claimed initial recognition of his friend's potential talent. *Outing's* first Remington illustration appeared in December of 1886. Yet an article in the *New York American* announced, "It is an interesting fact that Richard Watson Gilder, editor of the *Century Magazine* for many years . . . gave young Remington his first encouragement in the line of magazine illustration." [17] *Century's* first Remington illustration appeared in February of 1886.

Reminiscing to art critic Perriton Maxwell, Remington himself recounted that "my first commission was from *Harper's Weekly*. I did a picture based on an incident in the Geronimo campaign. That was in the early eighties. But let the poor thing rest. It was a very bad drawing, of course. I should rather not have it dragged from its well-deserved obscurity." [18] *Harper's* first Remington illustration appeared in February of 1882, and thirty-one others appeared therein before *Outing* or *Century* had reproduced their first.

Half of the first six sketches which Remington had submitted to *Harper's* were redrawn. The first was titled "Cow-boys of Arizona: Roused by a Scout" which was shown in the February 25, 1882 issue and redrawn by William A. Rogers. It is unlikely that Remington had been in Arizona by then, and his original sketch was apparently a Montana scene. However, Remington admitted to Rogers that "it was you who introduced me to the public. That was my first appearance and I was mighty glad I fell into the hands of an artist who knew a cowboy saddle and a Western horse." [19] His second illustration was "Ejecting an Oklahoma Boomer" in the March 28, 1885 issue, redrawn this time by Thure de Thulstrup. Remington might have witnessed the Boomers from his Kansas vantage. But his third published illustration, "The Apache War: Indian Scouts on Geronimo's Trail," was not redrawn. Appearing in the January 9, 1886 issue of *Harper's*, it stands as the first published illustration since his Yale days drawn exclusively by him.

Thulstrup also redrew Remington's sixth published illustration, "Shot on Picket." Many of this 1886 series were based on Remington's southwest trip and featured the Black 10th Cavalry. Few original sketches remain, but one watercolor in the Sid W. Richardson Foundation Collection in Fort Worth shows a Black cavalryman leading "The Riderless Horse." The wood engraving based on this watercolor depicts a white man and changes the feeling of the original. Montgomery Schuyler, managing editor for *Harper's* at that time, recalled that "Remington told me, long after, how he hated me bitterly for spoiling his copy. I agreed that Thulstrup had spoiled the drawing, taken all the 'race' and character out of it and made it 'very select and respectable and responsible and ridiculous.'" [20]

Remington's furor was understandable, perhaps augmented by his growing maturity as an illustrator. He did learn from Thulstrup in the way of form, especially fullness. Soon Remington was redrawing others' sketches, as the notation on an 1889 *Harper's* illustration revealed — "Drawn by Frederic Remington from a sketch by C. F. Holder."

Before the mid-1870s illustrators relied on wood engravers to reproduce their images. The graphic techniques used by *Harper's* and others involved taking the original wood block pattern and forming a mold. This matrix was then coated with a microscopic layer of graphite. Passing a direct electric current through the graphite layer in a solution of copper sulphate built a thin shell of copper, which was then backed with molten lead. After being planed down to a uniform thickness the resultant plate was ready for printing. This electrotype technique not only protected the original wood block, but also was more stable, especially in larger sizes where wood blocks would have had to have been bolted together.

Remington rejoiced in the advent of halftone printing and photographically processed blocks. These developments in the 1890s allowed areas of tonal gradations by the use of white flecks, dots or lines. "It has all the qualities of the original," he wrote Frederick B. Schell, an editor of *Harper's*, about a proof he had received. "It is one of those things that make an illustrator's life worth living. These engravers are all right when they do great work but they need a good deal of special dispensation to purge their sins. . . . The point of this letter is to let you know that I am happy — and there is no charge for all this information. . . ."[21]

Remington's field sketches were often done in watercolor, though he soon found that pen and ink made the work of the wood engravers easier and less likely to be distorted. He sometimes used old prints for copy material. For example, in the *Century Magazine* of April, 1902 appeared "First View of Salt Lake from a Mountain Pass," signed "Frederic Remington from an old lithograph '52." He also relied on the camera, as did many artists of his time. Later he abandoned its use. "I do not employ photography at all now, though I once found it a great help. . . . Photography when used judiciously is all right, but . . . there's the rub."[22] Remington had perceived a potential problem with a reliance on photographs. Joseph Pennell claimed that "photography killed Remington," declaring that his drawings had a "photographic look which mars all his work."[23]

Few were as critical as Pennell. Theodore Roosevelt actively sought Remington as the illustrator for a series of articles in the *Century Magazine* in 1888. "The thing which I like best," Remington wrote a friend in November of that year, "is a holiday book by Roosevelt — 'Ranch Life and The Hunting Trail' just issued by the 'Century Co.' and full of illustrations by myself."[24] Both author and artist were pleased with the collaboration, and a long friendship ensued between these two easterners whose energies and interests had much to do with the West.

By 1888 Remington had established himself as an illustrator in great demand. "Fred has as firm a grip on *Harper's* and the *Century* as any artist in this country," Missie wrote to his uncle, Horace Sackrider. "He has all he can do. *Harper's* if you notice is having something every week in the weekly — *Harper's* takes all he can make and asks no questions. . . . Fred is told by artists that he is talked about more than any artist in this country and everyone looks upon him as the strongest man."[25]

As an illustrator of the recent past, Remington believed that trips west were vital, both to be able to capture the proper milieu and to collect materials and incidents from which he could draw. For these reasons, his world of illustration had its trials. In a letter to Missie at the beginning of a summer trip through the Southwest in 1888, Remington related his various travails and concluded with a stubborn determination. "Well, all this is very discouraging but it's an artist's life. I have no idea how long this thing will take for these Indians are scattered all over the earth but I 'touch and go' and you can bet I won't spend the evening with them — still I came to do the wild tribes and I do it."[26]

As a pictorial war correspondent, Remington felt even greater anguish, perhaps due to the frustration of being an observer rather than a participant. "It is well to bear in mind the difference in the point of view of an artist or a correspondent, and a soldier. One has his duties, his responsibilities, or his gun, and he is on the firing-line under great excitement, with his reputation at stake. The other stalks through the middle distance, seeing the fight and its immediate results, the wounded; lying down by a dead body, mayhap, when the bullets come quickly; he will share no glory; he has only the responsibility of seeing clearly what he must tell; and he must keep his nerve. I think the soldier sleeps better nights."[27]

In spite of these trials, Remington stuck to his conviction that an illustrator had to be intimately familiar with the subject at hand. When asked to do some drawings of the Civil War, he replied in the negative. "The fact is that I do not do the Civil War period because I do not know enough about it. It is a mistake to think that I can handle that subject. I am weak enough at times to attempt things which I know little or nothing about, but if I ever give it a second thought I withdraw."[28] When asked to do a calendar by lithographer Louis Prang, Remington declined, frankly citing a deficiency in what was requested. "As to the calendar, I have thought it over and am inclined to doubt my ability — my instincts are not sufficiently decorative for the task."[29] In response to a letter of inquiry from the artist Maynard Dixon, he sent this advice: "Be always true to your self — to the way and the things you see in nature."[30]

More adamant was Remington about his preferences in subject matter — soldiers, cowboys, Indians, toughs, and never women. "'I never painted but one woman,' he said once, 'and I washed her out of the picture.'"[31]

Remington's renown as an illustrator is unquestioned. He was active during the golden age of American illustration, a field then "accepted as fine art in America. This may be accounted for," Barbara Rose explains, "by the egalitarian nature of our society, with its fixed traditions and its constant demands for an art that can be understood by the majority."[32]

Although Remington left the field of illustration for painting and sculpture, he firmly believed in the importance of his beginning work. "To be a successful illustrator," he once wrote, "is to be fully as much of a man as to be a successful painter. . . ."[33]

Remington devoted his career to a way of life which, he acknowledged, was quickly disappearing. The West — its people and scenery — gave him a focus for documentation and interpretation, and to the West he gave his life. While a more lasting fame awaited him in oil and bronze, Remington affected more people through his many wonderful illustrations. "It is a fact that admits of no question that Eastern people have formed their conceptions of what the Far-Western life is like, more from what they have seen in Mr. Remington's pictures than from any other source, and if they went to the West or to Mexico they would expect to see men and places looking exactly as Mr. Remington has drawn them. Those who have been there are authority for saying that they would not be disappointed."[34]

Peter H. Hassrick

INTRODUCTION FOOTNOTES

1. Julian Ralph, "Frederic Remington," *Harper's Weekly*, XXXIX (July 13, 1895), 688.
2. Letter from Frederic Remington to John Howard, dated Burlington, June 18, 1874 (?), St. Lawrence University Library, Canton, New York.
3. Orin E. Crooker, "A Page from the Boyhood of Frederic Remington: Some of the Earliest Concepts of the Painter of Adventure," *Collier's*, XLV (September 17, 1910), 28.
4. *Catalogue of the Officers and Students of Yale College, With a Statement of the course of Instruction in the Various Departments, 1878–1879* (New Haven, 1878), p. 72.
5. "College Riff-Raff," *The Yale Courant* (November 2, 1878), 47.
6. Poultney Bigelow, *Seventy Summers*, I, 301.
7. Pierre Remington, "Interesting and Unusual Points Relative to the Life of Frederick (sic) Remington," typescript in the Robert Taft Papers, Kansas State Historical Society, Topeka.
8. "When Remington Was In Albany," *The Albany Evening Journal*, December 28, 1909, p. 8.
9. Ibid.
10. Orison Sweet Marden (ed.), *Little Visits with Great Americans* (New York: The Success Company, 1905), p. 328.
11. *Kansas City Star*, January 23, 1891, p. 5.
12. "Dim Beginnings of Remington," *Kansas City Star*, February 5, 1911, p. 3B.
13. Mrs. Nellie Hough, "Remington at Twenty-Three," *International Studio*, LXXVI (February, 1923), 43.
14. Henry Harper, *The House of Harper* (New York: Harper, 1912), p. 603.
15. Letter from Frederic Remington to Grant Fitch, November 13, 1888, Milwaukee Art Center.
16. Frederic Remington 1886 Summer Journal, Robert Taft Papers.
17. "Artist Remington, Plainsman, Dies; Depicted History of the Old West," *New York American* (December 27, 1909), 11.
18. Perriton Maxwell, "Frederic Remington — Most Typical of American Artists," *Pearson's Magazine*, XVIII (October, 1907), 402.
19. William A. Rogers, *A World Worth While* (New York: Harper, 1922), p. 245.
20. Letter from Montgomery Schuyler to Johnson, January 20, 1910 (?), The Century Collection, Archives of American Art, Washington, D.C.
21. Letter from Frederic Remington to Frederick B. Schell, January 8, 1890, New York Historical Society, New York.
22. Maxwell, op. cit., 403.
23. Joseph Pennell, *Pen Drawing and Pen Draughtsmen* (London: T. Fisher Unwin Ltd., Publisher, 1921), p. 289.
24. Letter from F. Remington to G. Fitch, op. cit.
25. Letter from Missie Remington to Horace Sackrider, December 12, 1888, Robert Taft Papers.
26. Letter from Frederic Remington to Missie Remington, July, 1888, Robert Taft Papers.
27. Frederic Remington, *Men with the Bark On* (New York: Harper, 1900), p. 208.
28. Letter from Frederic Remington to Mr. Sparhawk, November 26, (?), The Historical Society of Pennsylvania.
29. Letter from Frederic Remington to Mr. L. Prang, December 13, (?), Manuscript Department, Lilly Library, Indiana University, Bloomington, Indiana.
30. Letter from Frederic Remington to Maynard Dixon, September 3, 1891, Rockwell Gallery, Corning, New York.
31. Orin E. Crooker, loc. cit.
32. Barbara Rose, *American Art Since 1900: A Critical History* (New York: Frederick A. Praeger, 1967), p. 8.
33. Letter from F. Remington to M. Dixon, op. cit.
34. William A. Coffin, "American Illustration of To-day," *Scribner's Magazine*, XI (March, 1892), 348.

THE FIRST EMIGRANT TRAIN TO CALIFORNIA

John Bidwell (Pioneer of '41)

ON THE WAY TO THE PLATTE

In May of 1841 our emigrant party struck out from Missouri to California. For a time, until we reached the Platte River, one day was much like another. We set forth every morning and camped every night, detailing men to stand guard. Captain Fitzpatrick and his party would generally take the lead and we would follow. Fitzpatrick knew all about the Indian tribes, and when there was any danger, we kept in a more compact body, to protect one another. At other times we would be scattered along, sometimes for half a mile or more. We were generally together, because there was often work to be done to avoid delay. We had to make the road, frequently digging down steep banks, filling gulches, and removing stones. In such cases everybody would take a spade or do something to help make the road passable.

ON THE WAY TO THE PLATTE

OUR WAY WEST

In general our route lay from Westport, where Kansas City now is, northwesterly over the prairie, crossing several streams, till we struck the Platte River. Then we followed along the south side of the Platte along the South Fork. Here the features of the country became more interesting. Then crossing the South Fork of the Platte, we went over the North Fork and camped at Ash Hollow; thence up the north side of that fork, passing those noted landmarks known as the Court House Rocks, Chimney Rock, and Scott's Bluffs. Soon we came to Fort Laramie, a trading post of the American Fur Company.

FORT LARAMIE IN 1849

AN EMIGRANT ENCAMPMENT

When we camped at night we usually drew the wagons and carts together in a hollow square and picketed our animals inside in the corral. The wagons were common ones and of no special pattern, and some of them were covered. The tongue of one would be fastened to the back of another. To lessen the danger from Indians, we usually had no fires at night and did our cooking in the daytime.

AN EMIGRANT ENCAMPMENT

A PERIL OF THE PLAINS

The first incident was a scare that we had from a party of Cheyenne Indians about two weeks after we set out. One of our men, who chanced to be out hunting, suddenly appeared without mule, gun, or pistol, and lacking most of his clothes. In great excitement, he reported that he had been surrounded by thousands of Indians. The company, too, became excited, and Captain Fitzpatrick tried, but with little success, to control and pacify them. Every man started his team into a run, till the oxen, like the mules and horses, were in a full gallop. Captain Fitzpatrick went ahead and directed them to follow, and as fast as they came to the bank of the river he put the wagons in a hollow square and had all the animals securely picketed within.

After a while the Indians came in sight. There were only forty of them, but they were well mounted on horses, and were evidently a war party, for they had no women except one, a medicine woman. They came up and camped within a hundred yards of us on the river below. Fitzpatrick told us that they would not have come in that way if they were hostile. When the Indians had put up their lodges, Fitzpatrick and the hunter went out to them and by signs were made to understand that the Indians did not intend to hurt him or to take his mule and gun, but that he was so agitated when he saw them that they had to disarm him to keep him from shooting them. They surrendered the mule and the gun, thus showing they were friendly. They proved to be Cheyenne Indians, and ever afterward that man went by the name of Cheyenne Dawson.

A PERIL OF THE PLAINS

SPLITTING THE HERD

I think I can truly say that I saw in that region more buffalo in one day than I have seen of cattle all my life. I have seen the plains black with them for several days' journey as far as the eye could reach. They seemed to be coming northward continually from the distant plains to the Platte to get water, and would plunge in and swim across by the thousands — so numerous were they that they changed not only the color of the water, but its taste, until it was unfit to drink.

One night when we were encamped on the South Fork of the Platte they came in such droves that we had to stay awake, shoot guns and make fires in order to keep them from running over us and trampling us into dust. We were obliged to go out some distance from camp to turn them, for if we did not do this the buffalo in front could not turn aside due to the pressure of those behind. We could hear them thundering all night long; the ground fairly trembled with their vast approaching bands. If they had not been diverted, wagons, animals, and emigrants would have been trodden under their feet. One cannot nowadays describe the rush and wildness of the thing.

A strange feature was that when old oxen, tired and foot-sore, got among a buffalo-herd, as they sometimes would in the night, they would soon become as wild as the wildest buffalo; and if ever recovered it was only because they could not run as fast as our horses.

DRY COUNTRY

As our party neared the Great Salt Lake, we sent four men ahead to reconnoiter. They brought back the information that we must strike out west of the Salt Lake — as it was even then called by the trappers — being careful not to go too far south, lest we should get into a broken waterless country and steep canyons, and wander about, as trapping parties had been known to do, and become bewildered and perish.

SPLITTING THE HERD

THIRSTY OXEN STAMPEDING FOR WATER

TO THE GREAT SALT LAKE

September had come before we reached the Salt Lake, which we struck at its northern extremity. Part of the time we had purposely traveled slowly to enable the men we had sent out to overtake us. But unavoidable delays were frequent: daily, often hourly, the road had to be made passable for our wagons. Indian fires obscured mountains and valleys in a dense, smoky atmosphere, so that we could not see for any considerable distance and thus avoid obstacles.

CROSSING WATER TO ESCAPE A PRAIRIE FIRE

WATER!

In search of water, we turned from a southerly to an easterly course, went about ten miles, and soon after daylight arrived at the Bear River. So near to Salt Lake were we that the water in the river was too salty for us or the animals to use, but we still had to use it. It would not quench thirst, but it did save life. The grass looked most luxuriant, and sparkled as if covered with frost. But it was salt: our hungry, jaded animals refused to eat it, and we had to lie by a whole day to rest them before we could travel.

One of the most serious of our troubles was to find water where we could camp at night. So soon after nightfall came another hot day, and hard travel all day and all night without water was an extreme privation.

WATER!

THE LAST LEG

We went on, traveling west as near as we could. When we killed our last ox we shot and ate crows, and one man shot a wildcat. We could eat anything. In search of food, I found myself at an enormous fallen tree — the butt seemed to be twenty or twenty-five feet over my head. This I suppose to have been one of the fallen trees in the Calaveras Grove of Sequoia gigantea, or mammoth trees. Once, two years later, I returned to that place, and concluded that I must have been the first white man who ever saw the Sequoia gigantea, of which I told Frémont when he came to California in 1844.

Our party — or rather, what was left of it — was now on the edge of the San Joaquin Valley, but we did not know that we were in California. We could see a range of mountains lying to the west, but could see no valley. The evening of the day we started into the valley we were very tired, and every man slept right where the darkness overtook him. He would take off his saddle for a pillow and turn his horse or mule loose — if he had one. His animal would be too weak to walk away, and in the morning he would find him, usually within fifty feet.

When we overtook the foremost of the party the next morning, we found they had come to a pond of water, and one of them had killed a fat coyote; when I came up it was all eaten except the lungs and the windpipe — on this I made my breakfast. But as soon as the Stanislaus River came in sight, we saw an abundance of antelope and sandhill cranes. We killed two of each the first evening there.

In a few more days we finally arrived at the first settlement in California. It was November 4, 1841: six months after we left Missouri.

ABANDONED

HORSES OF THE PLAINS

Frederic Remington

A TEXAN PONY

The most inexperienced horseman will not have to walk around the animal twice in order to tell a Texas pony; that is, one which is full bred, with no admixture. He has fine deer-like legs, a very long body, with a pronounced roach just forward of the coupling, and possibly a "glass eye" and a pinto hide. Any old cowboy will point him out as the only creature suitable for his purposes. Hard to break, because he has any amount of latent devil in his disposition, he does not break his legs or fall over backwards in the "pitching" process as does the "cayuse" of the Northwest. I think he is small and shriveled up like a Mexican horse because of his dry, hot habitat, over which he has to walk many miles to get his dinner. But, in compensation, he can cover leagues of his native plains, bearing a seemingly disproportionately large man, with an ease both to himself and his rider which is little short of miraculous.

A "CAYUSE"

The cayuse is generally roan in color, with always a tendency this way, no matter how slight. He is strongly built, heavily muscled, and the only bronco that possesses square quarters. In height he is about fourteen hands; and while not possessed of the activity of the Texas horse, he has much more power. This native stock was a splendid foundation for the horse-breeders of Montana and the Northwest to work on, and the Montana horse of commerce rates very high. This condition is not, however, all to the credit of the cayuse, but to a strain of horses early imported into Montana from the West and known as the Oregon horse, which breed had its foundation in the mustang.

A TEXAN PONY

A "CAYUSE"

BRONCOS AND TIMBER WOLVES

I tried on one occasion to regenerate a fine specimen of the southern plains sort, and to make a pretty little cob out of the wild, scared bundle of nerves and bones which I had picked out of a herd. I roached his mane and docked his tail, and put him in a warm stall with half a foot of straw underneath. I meted out a ration of corn and hay which was enough for a twelve-hundred pound work-horse in the neighboring stall. I had him combed and brushed and wiped by a good-natured man, who regarded the proceeding with as much awe as did the pony. After the animal found out that the corn was meant to be eaten, he always ate it; but after many days he was led out, and, to my utter despair, he stood there the same shy, perverse brute which he had always been. His paunch was distended to frightful proportions, but his cat hams, ewe neck, and thin little shoulders were as dry and hard as ever. Mentally he never seemed to make any discrimination between his newly found masters and the big timber wolves that used to surround him and keep him standing all night in a bunch of fellows. On the whole it was laughable, for in his perversity he resisted the regenerating process much as any other wild beast might.

BRONCOS AND TIMBER WOLVES

PONIES PAWING IN THE SNOW

Unless he be tied up to a post, no one ever knew an Indian pony to die of the cold. With his front feet he will paw away the snow to an astonishing depth in order to get at the dry herbage, and by hook or by crook he will manage to come through the winter despite the wildest prophecies on the part of the uninitiated that he cannot live ten days in such a storm.

HORSE OF THE CANADIAN NORTHWEST

As we go very far into the Canadian Northwest we find the interminable cold of the winters has had its effect, and the pony is small and scraggy, with a disposition to run to hair that would be the envy of a goat. These little fellows seem to be sadly out of their reckoning, as the great northern wastes were surely not made for horses; however, the reverse of the proposition is true, for the horses thrive after a fashion and demonstrate the toughness of the race.

The Indian pony often finds to his sorrow that he is useful for other purposes than as a beast of burden, for his wild masters of the Rocky Mountains think him excellent eating. To the Shoshones the particular use of a horse was for the steaks and stews that were in him; but the Indian of the plains had the buffalo and could afford, except in extreme cases, to let his means of transportation live.

PONIES PAWING IN THE SNOW

HORSE OF THE CANADIAN NORTHWEST

SPANISH HORSE OF NORTHERN MEXICO

One thing is certain: of all the monuments which the Spaniard has left to glorify his reign in America there will be none more worthy than his horse. The Spaniard's horses may be found today in countless thousands, from the city of the Montezumas to the regions of perpetual snow; they are grafted into our equine wealth and make an important impression on the horse of the country.

A BRONCO IN CENTRAL PARK

In summing up for the bronco I will say that he is destined to become a distinguished element in the future horse of the continent, if for no other reason except that of his numbers. All over the West he is bred into the stock of his country, and of course always from the side of the dam. The first one or two crosses from this stock are not very encouraging, as the blood is strong, having been bred in and in for so many generations. But presently we find an animal of the average size, as fine almost as a thoroughbred, with his structural points corrected, and fit for many purposes. He has about the general balance of the French ponies of Canada or perhaps a Morgan, which for practical purposes were the best horses ever developed in America. At this stage of the development of the bronco he is no longer the little narrow-shouldered, cat-hammered brute of his native plains, but as round and square and arched as "anybody's horse," as a Texan would express it. In this shape I see him ridden in Central Park, and fail to see but that he carries himself as gallantly as though his name were in the "Stud-Book."

SPANISH HORSE OF NORTHERN MEXICO   A BRONCO IN CENTRAL PARK

THE HOME RANCH

Theodore Roosevelt

IN WITH THE HORSE HERD

A ranchman's life is certainly a pleasant one, albeit generally varied with plenty of hardship and anxiety. Although occasionally he passes days of severe toil, he no longer has to undergo the monotonous drudgery attendant upon the tasks of the cowboy or of the apprentice in the business.

Each of us has his own string of horses, eight or ten in number, and the whole band is usually split up into two or three companies. Once every two or three days somebody rides round and finds out where each of these smaller bands is, but the man who goes out in the morning merely gathers one bunch. He drives these into one corral, the other men (who have been lolling idly about the house or stable, fixing their saddles or doing an odd job) coming out with their ropes as soon as they hear the patter of the unshod hoofs and the shouts of the cowboy driver.

IN WITH THE HORSE HERD

ROPING IN A HORSE-CORRAL

Going into the corral, and standing near the center, each of us picks out some of his own string from among the animals that are trotting and running in a compact mass around the circle; and after one or more trials, according to his skill, ropes it and leads it out. When all have caught their horses, the rest are turned loose, together with those that have been kept up overnight. Some horses soon get tame and do not need to be roped; my pet cutting pony, little Muley, and good old Manitou, my companion on so many hunting trips, will neither of them stay with the rest of their fellows that are jamming and jostling each other as they rush round in the dust of the corral, but they very sensibly walk up and stand quietly with the men in the middle, by the snubbing-post. Both are great pets, Manitou in particular; the wise old fellow being very fond of bread and sometimes coming up of his own accord to the ranch house and even putting his head in the door to beg for it.

ROPING IN A HORSE-CORRAL

IN A BOG-HOLE

During the early spring months, before the round-up begins, the chief work is in hauling out mired cows and steers; and if we did not keep a sharp lookout, the losses at this season would be very serious. As long as everything is frozen solid there is, of course, no danger from miring; but when the thaw comes, along towards the beginning of March, a period of new danger sets in. When the ice breaks up, the streams are left with an edging of deep bog, while the quicksand is at its worst. As the frost goes out of the soil, the ground round every little alkali-spring changes into a trembling quagmire, and deep holes of slimy, treacherous mud form in the bottom of all the gullies. An alkali-hole, where the water oozes out through the thick clay, is the worst of all, owing to the ropy tenacity with which the horrible substance sticks and clings to any unfortunate beast that gets into it.

A DEEP FORD

When the river is up it is a very common thing for a horseman to have great difficulty in crossing, for the swift, brown water runs over a bed of deep quicksand that is ever shifting. An inexperienced horse or a mule—for a mule is useless in mud or quicksand—becomes mad with fright in such a crossing, and, after speedily exhausting its strength in wild struggles, will throw itself on its side and drown unless the rider gets it out. An old horse used to such work will, on the contrary, take matters quietly and often push along through really dangerous quicksand. Old Manitou never loses his head for an instant; but, now resting a few seconds, now feeling his way cautiously forward, and now making two or three desperate plunges, will go on wherever a horse possibly can.

A DEEP FORD   IN A BOG-HOLE

THE MIDDAY MEAL

The long forenoon's work, with its attendant mishaps to man and beast, being over, the men who have been out among the horses and cattle come riding in, to be joined by their fellows who have been hunting, or haying, or chopping wood. The midday dinner is variable as to time, for it comes when the men have returned from their work; but, whatever be the hour, it is the most substantial meal of the day, and we feel that we have little fault to find with a table on whose clean cloth are spread platters of smoked elk meat, loaves of good bread, jugs and bowls of milk, saddles of venison or broiled antelope steaks, perhaps roast and fried prairie chickens, with eggs, butter, wild plums, and tea or coffee.

THE MIDDAY MEAL

A BUCKING BRONCO

A first-class flash rider or bronco-buster receives high wages and deserves them, for he follows a most dangerous trade, at which no man can hope to grow old. A bronco-buster has to work by such violent methods in consequence of the short amount of time at his command. Horses are cheap, each outfit has a great many, and the wages for breaking an animal are but five or ten dollars. Three rides, of an hour or two each, on as many consecutive days, are the outside number a bronco-buster deems necessary before turning an animal over as "broken."

CRUISING FOR STOCK

In making a journey over ground we know, during the hot weather we often prefer to ride by moonlight. After nightfall the face of the country seems to alter marvelously, and the cool moonlight only intensifies the change. The river gleams like running quicksilver, and the moonbeams play over the grassy stretches of the plateaus and glance off the wind-rippled blades as they would from water. The Bad Lands seem to be stranger and wilder than ever, the silvery waves turning the country into a kind of grim fairy-land. The grotesque, fantastic outlines of the higher cliffs stand out with startling clearness, while the lower buttes have become formless, misshapen masses, and the deep gorges are in black shadow; in the darkness there will be no sound but the rhythmic echo of the hoof-beats of the horses, and the steady, metallic clank of the steel bridle-chains.

A BUCKING BRONCO

CRUISING FOR STOCK

LINE RIDING IN WINTER

The men in the line camps lead a hard life, for they have to be out in every kind of weather, and should be especially active and watchful during the storms. The camps are established along some line which it is proposed to make the boundary of the cattle's drift in a given direction. Line riding is very cold work, and dangerous too, when the men have to be out in a blinding snowstorm, or in a savage blizzard that takes the spirit in the thermometer far down below zero. In the worst storms it is impossible for any man to be out.

THE OUTLYING CAMP

The line camps are usually for two men each, and some fifteen or twenty miles apart. In the morning, its two men start out in opposite ways, each riding till he meets his neighbor of the next camp nearest on that side, and then returns. The camp itself is sometimes merely a tent pitched in a sheltered coulee, but ought to be made of logs or else a dug-out in the ground. A small corral and horse-shed is near by, with enough hay for the ponies, of which each rider has two or three.

THE OUTLYING CAMP

LINE RIDING IN WINTER

CATTLE DRIFTING BEFORE THE STORM

In riding over the beat each man drives any cattle that have come near it back into the Bad Lands, and if he sees by the hoof-marks that a few have strayed out over the line very recently, he will follow and fetch them home. They must be shoved well back into the Bad Lands before a great storm strikes them; for if they once begin to drift in masses before an icy gale it is impossible for a small number of men to hold them, and the only thing is to let them go, and to organize an expedition to follow them as soon as possible.

CATTLE DRIFTING BEFORE THE STORM

THE HOMECOMING

In the winter there is much less work than in any other season, but what there is involves great hardship and exposure. Many of the men are discharged after the summer is over, and during much of the cold weather there is little to do except hunt now and then, and in very bitter days lounge about the house.

There are few moments more pleasant than the homecoming, when, in the gathering darkness, after crossing the last chain of ice-covered buttes, or after coming round the last turn in the wind-swept valley, we see the red gleam of the firelight as it shines through the ranch windows and flickers over the trunks of the cottonwoods outside, warming a man's blood by the mere hint of the warmth awaiting him within.

THANKSGIVING DINNER FOR THE RANCH

Frederic Remington
J '88
Arizona-

A SCOUT WITH THE BUFFALO SOLDIERS

Frederic Remington

LIEUTENANT CARTER P. JOHNSON

I sat smoking in the quarters of an army friend at Fort Grant, and through a green lattice-work was watching the dusty parade and congratulating myself on the possession of this spot of comfort in such a disagreeably hot climate as Arizona Territory offers in the summer, when in strode my friend the lieutenant, who threw his cap on the table and began to roll a cigarette.

"Well," he said, "the K. O. has ordered me out for a two-weeks' scouting up the San Carlos way, and I'm off in the morning. Would you like to go with me?" He lighted the cigarette and paused for my reply.

I very much desired to travel through the country to the north, and in a rash moment said, "I'll go."

"You quite understand that you are amenable to discipline," continued the lieutenant with mock seriousness, as he regarded me with that soldier's contempt for a citizen which is not openly expressed but is tacitly felt.

"I do," I answered meekly.

"Put you afoot, citizen; put you afoot, sir, at the slightest provocation, understand," pursued the officer in his sharp manner of giving commands.

I suggested that after I had chafed a Government saddle for a day or two I should undoubtedly beg to be put afoot, and, far from being a punishment, it might be a real mercy.

"That being settled, will you go down to stable-call and pick out a mount? You are one of the heavies, but I think we can outfit you," he said; and together we strolled down to where the bugle was blaring.

LIEUTENANT CARTER P. JOHNSON

RECREATIONS OF A "MOUNTED INFANTRYMAN"

At the adobe corral the faded coats of the horses were being groomed by black troopers in white frocks; for the 10th United States Cavalry is composed of colored men. A fine old veteran cavalry horse, detailed for a sergeant of the troop, was selected to bear me on the trip. He was a large horse of the pony build, both strong and sound except that he bore a healed-up saddle-gall, gotten, probably, during some old march on an endless Apache trail. His temper had been ruined, said a grinning soldier.

The lieutenant assured me that if I could ride that animal and not start the old gall I should be covered in glory; and as to the rest, "What you don't know about riding in these parts that horse does. It's lucky there isn't a hole in the ground where his hoofs trod, for he's pounded up and down across this Territory for the last five years."

THE PATIENT PACK-MULE

Presently we halted and dismounted to tighten the packs, which work loose after the first hour. One by one the packers caught the little mules, threw a blind over their eyes, and "Now, Whitey! Ready! eve-e-e-e — gimme that loop! " came from the men as they heaved and tossed the circling ropes in the mystic movements of the diamond hitch. "All fast, Lieutenant," cries a packer, and mounting we move on up the long slope of the mesa towards the Sierras.

THE PATIENT PACK-MULE

RECREATIONS OF A "MOUNTED INFANTRYMAN"

WATCHING THE APACHE

In obedience to an order of the department commander, General Miles, scouting parties like ours are constantly being sent out from the chain of forts which surround the great San Carlos reservation. The purpose is to make provision against Apache outbreaks, which are momentarily expected, by familiarizing officers and soldiers with the vast solitude of mountain and desert. New trails for the movement of cavalry columns across the mountains are threaded out, waterholes of which the soldiers have no previous knowledge are discovered, and an Apache band is at all times liable to meet a cavalry command in out-of-the-way places.

INFANTRYMAN IN FIELD COSTUME   APACHE SIGNAL FIRE

MARCHING ON THE MOUNTAINS

After a needed rest, we began the descent on the other side of the mountain. This was a new experience. The prospect of being suddenly overwhelmed by an avalanche of horse-flesh as the result of some unlucky stumble makes the recruit constantly apprehensive. But the trained horses are sure of foot, understand the business, and seldom stumble except when treacherous ground gives way.

A POOL IN THE DESERT

Once we were forced to make a "dry camp"; that is, one where no water is to be found. There is such an amount of misery locked up in the thought of a dry camp that I refuse to dwell on it. We were glad enough to get upon the trail in the morning, and in time found a nice running mountain-brook. The command wallowed in it. We drank as much as we could and then sat down. We arose and drank some more, and yet we drank again, and still once more, until we were literally water-logged.

A POOL IN THE DESERT

MARCHING ON THE MOUNTAINS

MARCHING IN THE DESERT

I feel enough interested in the discomforts of the march to tell about it, but I find that there are not resources in any vocabulary. If the impression is abroad that a cavalry soldier's life in the Southwest has any of the lawn-party element in it, I think the impression could be effaced by doing a march like that. The great clouds of dust choke you and settle over horse, soldier, and accouterments until all local color is lost and black man and white man wear a common hue. The "chug, chug, chug" of your tired horse as he marches along becomes infinitely tiresome, and cavalry soldiers never ease themselves in the saddle. That is an army axiom.

MARCHING IN THE DESERT

THE MEN AND THEIR MOUNTS

No pains are spared to prolong the usefulness of an army horse, and every old soldier knows that his good care will tell when the long forced march comes some day, and when to be put afoot by a poor mount means great danger in Indian warfare. The soldier will steal for his horse, will share his camp bread, and will moisten the horse's nostrils and lips with the precious water in the canteen. In garrison the troop-horses lead a life of ease and plenty; but it is varied at times by a pursuit of hostiles, when they are forced over the hot sands and up over the perilous mountains all day long, only to see the sun go down with the rider still spurring them on amid the quiet of the long night.

IN THE DESERT

ONE OF THE REAL HEROES OF HARD MARCHING

"LAYING BACK" ON THE TRAIL

A RETIRING SCOUT

A TUMBLE FROM THE TRAIL

In course of time I came up with the command, which had stopped at a ledge so steep that it had daunted even these mountaineers. It was only a hundred-foot drop, and they presently found a place to go down, where, as one soldier suggested, "there isn't footing for a lizard." On, on we go, when suddenly with a great crash some sandy ground gives way, and a collection of hoofs, troop-boots, ropes, canteens, and flying stirrups goes rolling over in a cloud of dust and finds a lodgement in the bottom of a dry watercourse. The dust settles and discloses a soldier and his horse. They rise to their feet and appear astonished, but as the soldier mounts and follows on we know he is unhurt.

In due time the march continued without particular incident, and at last the scout "pulled in" to the home post, and I again sat in my easy-chair behind the lattice-work, firm in the conviction that soldiers, like other men, find more hard work than glory in their calling.

A TUMBLE FROM THE TRAIL

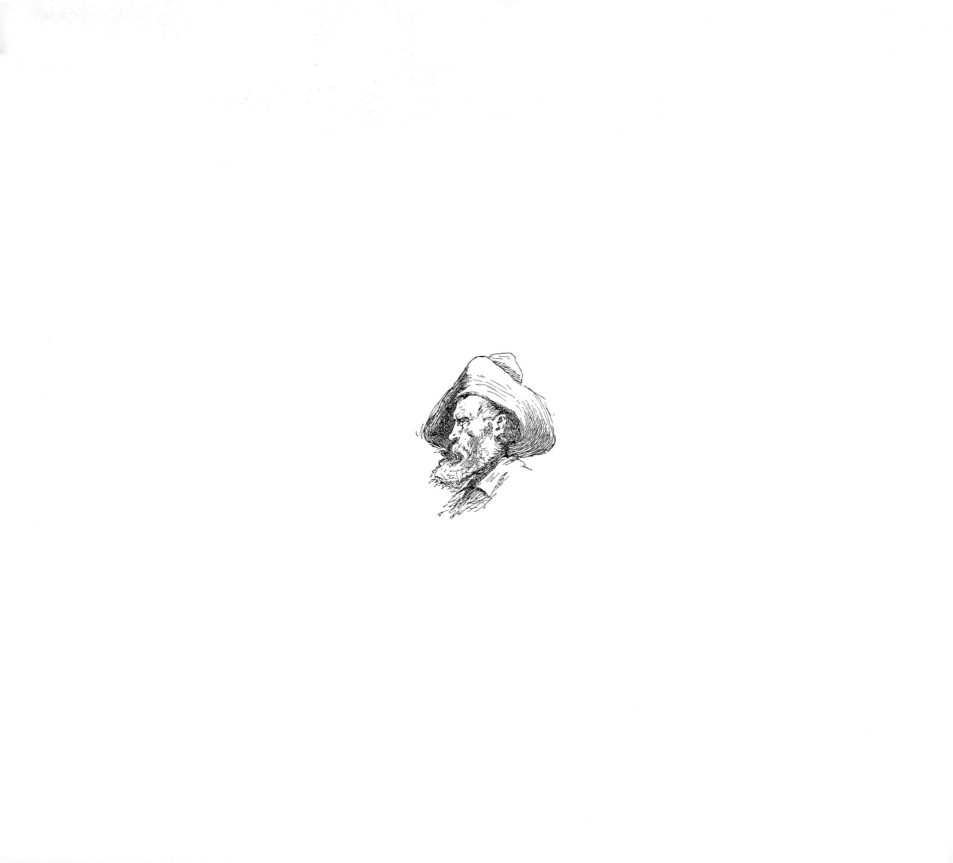

FRONTIER TYPES

Theodore Roosevelt

COWBOY DIVERSIONS

In the main, cowboys are good men; and the disturbance they cause in a town is done from sheer rough light-heartedness. They shoot off boot-heels or tall hats occasionally, or make some obnoxious butt "dance" by shooting round his feet; but they rarely meddle in this way with men who have not themselves played the fool. A fight in the streets is almost always a duel between two men who bear each other malice; it is only in a general melee in a saloon that outsiders often get hurt, and then it is their own fault, for they have no business to be there. One evening at Medora a cowboy spurred his horse up the steps of a rickety hotel piazza into the bar-room, where he began firing at the clock, the decanters, and the mirror behind the bar. The bartender took a shot at him, but missed. When he had emptied his revolver, he threw down a roll of banknotes on the counter to pay for the damage he had done, and galloped his horse out through the door, disappearing into the darkness with loud yells to a rattling accompaniment of pistol-shots.

A SUNDAY AFTERNOON SPORT

THE GAMBLER

The gambler, with hawk eyes and lissom fingers, is scarcely classed as a criminal; indeed, he may be a very public-spirited citizen. But since his trade is so often plied in saloons, he is of necessity obliged to be skillful and ready with his weapon, and gambling rows are very common: if he does not cheat, many of his opponents are certain to attempt to do so.

Cowboys lose much of their money to gamblers; it is with them hard come and light go, for they exchange the wages of six months' grinding toil and lonely peril for three days' whooping carousal, spending their money on poisonous whiskey or losing it over greasy cards in the vile dance houses.

A QUARREL OVER CARDS — A SKETCH FROM A NEW MEXICAN RANCH

A FUGITIVE

Horse-thieves are always numerous and formidable on the frontier; though in our own country they have been summarily thinned out of late years. Horses are the most valuable property of the frontiersman, whether cowboy, hunter, or settler, and are often absolutely essential to his well-being, and even to his life. They are always marketable, and are very easily stolen, for they carry themselves off instead of having to be carried. Horse-stealing is thus a most tempting business, especially to the more reckless ruffians, and it is always followed by armed men; and they can only be kept in check by ruthless severity. Frequently they band together with the road agents (highwaymen) and other desperadoes into secret organizations, which control and terrorize a district until overthrown by force.

After the Civil War a great many guerrillas, notably from Arkansas and Missouri, went out to the plains, often driving northward. They took naturally to horse-stealing and other kindred pursuits. Since I have been in the northern cattle country I have known of half a dozen former members of Quantrell's gang being hanged or shot.

A FUGITIVE

AN INCIDENT IN A SALOON

One curious shooting scrape took place in Medora that was worthy of being chronicled by Bret Harte. It occurred in the summer of 1884, I believe, but it may have been the year following. I did not see the actual occurrence, but I saw both men immediately afterwards; and I heard the shooting, which took place in a saloon. I will not give their full names, as I am not certain what has become of them; though I was told that one had since been put in jail or hanged, I forget which. One of them was a saloon-keeper, familiarly called Welshy. The other man, Hay, had been bickering with him for some time. One day Hay was out of temper, entered the other's saloon, and became very abusive. The quarrel grew more and more violent, and suddenly Welshy whipped out his revolver and blazed away at Hay. The latter staggered slightly, shook himself, stretched out his hand, and gave back to his would-be slayer the ball, saying, "Here, man, here's the bullet." It had glanced along his breast-bone, gone into his body, and came out at the point of the shoulder, when, being spent, it dropped down the sleeve into his hand.

"WHAT KIND OF JUSTICE DO YOU WANT?"

A ROW IN A CATTLE TOWN

Sometimes we had a comic row. There was one huge man from Missouri called "The Pike," who had been the keeper of a woodyard for steamboats on the Upper Missouri. Like most of his class, he was a hard case; and, though pleasant enough when sober, always insisted on fighting when drunk. One day, when on a spree, he announced his intention of thrashing the entire population of Medora one at a time, and began to make his promise good with great vigor and praiseworthy impartiality. He was victorious over the first two or three eminent citizens, but then tackled a gentleman known as "Cold Turkey Bill." Under ordinary circumstances Cold Turkey, though an able-bodied man, was no match for The Pike; but the latter was still rather drunk, and moreover was wearied by his previous combats.

So Cold Turkey got him down, lay on him, choked him by the throat with one hand, and began pounding his face with a triangular rock held in the other. To the onlookers the fate of the battle seemed decided; but Cold Turkey better appreciated the endurance of The Pike, and it soon appeared that he sympathized with the traditional hunter who, having caught a wildcat, earnestly besought a comrade to help him let it go. While still pounding vigorously, Cold Turkey raised an agonized wail: "Help me off, fellows, for the Lord's sake; he's tiring me out!"

A ROW IN A CATTLE-TOWN

LIFE IN THE SADDLE

But all these things are merely incidents in a cowboy's life. It is utterly unfair to judge the whole class by what a few individuals do in the course of two or three days spent in town, instead of by the long months of weary, honest toil common to all alike. To appreciate properly his fine, manly qualities, the wild rough-rider of the plains should be seen in his own home. There he passes his days; there he does his life-work; there, when he meets death, he faces it as he has faced many other evils, with quiet, uncomplaining fortitude. Brave, hospitable, hardy, and adventurous, he is the grim pioneer of our race; he prepares the way for the civilization from before whose face he must himself disappear. Hard and dangerous though his existence is, it has yet a wild attraction that strongly draws to it his bold, free spirit. He lives in the lonely lands where mighty rivers twist in long reaches between the barren bluffs; where the prairies stretch out into billowy plains of waving grass, girt only by the blue horizon — plains across whose endless breadth he can steer his course for days and weeks and see neither man to speak to nor hill to break the level; where the glory and the burning splendor of the sunset kindle the blue vault of heaven and the level brown earth till they merge together in an ocean of flaming fire.

IN FROM THE NIGHT HERD

THE SUN-DANCE OF THE SIOUX

Frederick Schwatka

GOING TO THE DANCE

It was in June that the celebration was to be held, and for many days before the first ceremonies took place the children of the prairies began to assemble, not only from the two agencies most interested, but from the many distant bands of Sioux to which rumors of the importance of this meeting had gone. Everywhere upon the plains were picturesque little caravans moving towards the level stretch between the branches of the Chadron — ponies dragging the lodge-poles of the tepees, with roughly constructed willow baskets hanging from the poles and filled with a confusion of pots and puppies, babies and drums, scalps and kindling-wood and rolls of jerked buffalo-meat, with old hags urging on the ponies, and gay young warriors riding. Fully twenty thousand Sioux were present when the opening day arrived. It was easier to believe the statement of the Indians that it was the grandest sun-dance within the memory of the oldest warriors, and I soon became convinced of this assertion.

GOING TO THE DANCE

THE SUN-POLE

When all had assembled and the medicine-men had set the day for the beginning of the great dance dedicated to the sun, the sun-pole was selected. A handsome young pine or fir, forty or fifty feet high, with the straightest and most uniformly tapering trunk that could be found within a reasonable distance, was chosen. The selection is always made by some old woman, generally the oldest one in the camp, who leads a number of maidens gaily dressed in the beautiful buckskin gowns they wear on state occasions. The part of the maidens is to strip the tree of its limbs as high as possible without felling it.

The selection of the tree is the only special feature of the first day's celebration. After it is stripped of its branches nearly to the top, the brushwood and trees for a considerable distance about it are removed, and it is left standing for the ceremony of the second day.

HERALDING THE SUNRISE

Long before sunrise the eager participants in the next great step were preparing themselves for the ordeal; and a quarter of an hour before the sun rose above the broken hills of white clay a long line of naked young warriors, in gorgeous war-paint and feathers, with rifles, bows, and arrows, and war-lances in hand, faced the east and the sun-pole, which was from five to six hundred yards away. Ordinarily this group of warriors numbers from fifty to possibly two hundred men. An interpreter near me estimated that the line I beheld was from a thousand to twelve hundred strong.

PAINTING THE ROBE

HERALDING THE SUNRISE

"MEDICINE ELK"

Not far away, on a high hill overlooking the scene, was a medicine-man of the tribe, whose solemn duty was to announce by a shout the exact moment when the tip of the morning sun appeared above the eastern hills. Perfect quiet rested upon the line of young warriors and upon the throng of spectators that blackened the green hills overlooking the arena. Suddenly the old warrior, who had been kneeling on one knee, with his extended palm shading his scraggy eyebrows, arose to his full height, and in a slow, dignified manner waved his blanketed arm above his head. The few warriors who were still unmounted now jumped hurriedly upon their ponies; the broken, wavering line rapidly took on a more regular appearance; and then the old man, who had gathered himself for the great effort, hurled forth a yell that could be heard to the uttermost limits of the great throng. The morning sun had sent its commands to its warriors on earth to charge.

"MEDICINE ELK"

THE CHARGE ON THE SUN-POLE

The shout from the hill was re-echoed by the thousand men in the valley; it was caught up by the spectators on the hills as the long line of warriors hurled themselves forward to the sun-pole, the objective point of every armed and naked Indian in the yelling line. As they converged upon it the slower ponies dropped out, and the weaker ones were crushed to the rear. Nearer and nearer they came, the long line becoming massed until it was but a surging crowd of plunging horses and yelling, gesticulating riders. When the leading warriors had reached a point within a hundred yards of the sun-pole, a sharp report of rifles sounded along the line, and a moment later the rushing mass was a sheet of flame, and the rattle of rifle-shots was like the rapid beat of a drum resounding among the hills. Every shot, every arrow, and every lance was directed at the pole, and bark and chips were flying from its sides like shavings from the rotary bit of a planer. When every bullet had been discharged, and every arrow and lance had been hurled, the riders crowded around the pole and shouted as only excited Indians can shout.

Later in the day the sun-pole was cut down and taken to the center of the great plain between the two forks of the Chadron, about a mile away. Here a slight excavation was made, and into it the butt of the sun-pole was set (the bushy top having now disappeared). Later it would be held upright by a number of ropes made from buffalo thongs converging from its top. Sometimes canvas, blankets, and light elkskins are thrown over these supporting ropes to ward off the fierce rays of the noonday sun.

THE CHARGE ON THE SUN-POLE

THE START OF THE SUN-DANCE

On the third day the sun-dance began. Within the arena were from six to twelve young warriors, still in war-costume of paint and feathers, standing in a row, and always facing the sun, however brightly it shone in their eyes. With fists clenched across the breast, like a foot-racer in a contest of speed, they jumped up and down in measured leaps to the monotonous beating of the tom-toms and the accompanying yi-yi-yi-yis of the assembled throng. Now and then a similar row of young maidens would appear in another part of the arena, and their soprano voices would break in pleasantly on the harsher voices of the men. The dancing continued for intervals of from ten minutes to a quarter of an hour, broken by rests of about equal length, and lasted from sunrise to sunset.

Many trifling ceremonies took place while the important ones were proceeding. Horses and ponies were brought into the arena, and the medicine-men, with incantations, dipped their hands into colored earth and besmeared the sides of the animals with it. As these animals were evidently the best war-ponies, the ceremony was doubtless a blessing or a consecration to war.

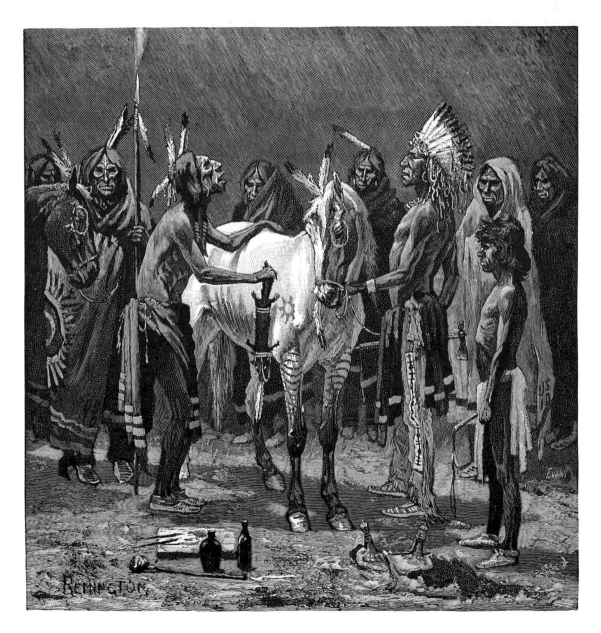

MAKING MEDICINE-PONIES

THE TORTURE

On the fourth day of the sun-dance the self-torture began, and I was told that those who were to submit themselves to the great ordeal were the same young warriors who had been dancing the day before.

Each one of the young men presented himself to a medicine-man, who took between his thumb and forefinger a fold of the loose skin of the breast, about halfway between the nipple and the collar-bone, lifted it as high as possible, and then ran a very narrow-bladed but sharp knife through the skin underneath the hand. Then a strong skewer of bone was inserted, and over its projections was thrown a figure-of-eight noose with a strong thong of dressed skin. This was tied to a long skin rope fastened, at its other extremity, to the top of the sun-pole in the center of the arena. The whole object of the devotee is to break loose from these fetters. To liberate himself he must tear the skewers through the skin, a horrible task that even with the most resolute may require several hours of torture. His first attempts are very easy, and seem intended to get him used to the horrible pain he must yet endure before he breaks loose from the thongs. As he increases his efforts his shouts increase, huge drops of perspiration pour down his greasy, painted skin, and every muscle stands out on his body in tortuous ridges. His swaying frame, as he throws his whole weight wildly against the fearful fetters, is convulsed with shudders. All the while the beating of the tom-toms and the wild, weird chanting of the singers near him continue.

THE ORDEAL IN THE SUN-DANCE AMONG THE BLACKFEET INDIANS

FACING THE SETTING SUN

When the day is almost over, and the solar deity is nearly down in the west, the self-tortured warriors file from the inclosed arena, one by one, and just outside the doors, richly covered with handsomely painted buffalo-robes, they kneel, and with arms crossed over their bloody breasts and with bowed heads face the setting sun and rise only when it has disappeared.

I will add that this sun-dance was called the greatest sun-dance the Sioux had ever held: the greatest self-sacrifice of the greatest nation within our boundaries. Within a year they had checked, at the Rosebud Hills in Montana, the largest army we had ever launched against the American Indians in a single fight, and then retired successfully to the Little Big Horn, a few miles away. There, a week later, they had wiped Custer's fine command from the face of the earth.

FACING THE SETTING SUN

THE ROUND-UP

Theodore Roosevelt

THE ROUND-UP

On cow-ranches, or wherever there is breeding-stock, the spring round-up is the great event of the season, as it is then that the bulk of the calves are branded. It usually lasts six weeks, or thereabouts; but its end by no means implies rest for the stockman. On the contrary, as soon as it is over, wagons are sent to work out-of-the-way parts of the country that have been passed over, but where cattle are supposed to have drifted; and by the time these have come back the first beef round-up has begun, and thereafter beeves are steadily gathered and shipped, at least from among the larger herds, until the cold weather sets in; and in the fall there is another round-up, to brand the late calves and see that the stock is got back on the range.

THE ROUND-UP

THE ASSOCIATION

The stock-growers of Montana, of the western part of Dakota, and even of portions of extreme northern Wyoming have united, and formed themselves into the great Montana Stock-Grower's Association. At the spring meeting of the Association, the entire territory mentioned above, including perhaps one hundred thousand square miles, is mapped out into round-up districts, which are slightly changed from year to year, so that the round-ups of adjacent districts may be run with a view to the best interests of all. Thus the stockmen along the Yellowstone have one round-up; we along the Little Missouri have another, and the country lying between, through which the Big Beaver flows, is almost equally important to both.

DRIVING TO THE ROUND-UP

At the appointed day all meet at the place from which the round-up is to start. If the starting-point is some distance off, it may be necessary to leave home three or four days in advance. Before this we have got everything in readiness; have overhauled the wagons, shod any horse whose forefeet are tender, and left things in order at the ranch. While traveling to the meeting-point the pace is always slow, as it is an object to bring the horses on the ground as fresh as possible. There is always some trouble with the animals at the starting out, as they are very fresh and restive under the saddle. The herd is likely to stampede, and any beast that is frisky or vicious is sure to show its worst side.

DRIVING TO THE ROUND-UP

AN EXPLORING OUTFIT

TRAILING CATTLE

"Trail" work is most important. Cattle, while driven from one range to another, or to a shipping point for beef, are said to be "on the trail." Such cattle, for the most part, once went along tolerably well-marked trails, which became for the time being of great importance. With the growth of the railroad system, and above all with the filling-up of the northern ranges, these trails have steadily become of less and less consequence. The trail work is something by itself. The herds may be on the trail several months, averaging fifteen miles or less a day. The foreman of a trail outfit must be not only a veteran cowhand, but also a miracle of patience and resolution.

THE HERD AT NIGHT

From 8 in the evening till 4 in the morning the day herd becomes a night herd. The first guards have to bed the cattle down, though the day-herders often do this themselves: it simply consists in hemming them into as small a space as possible, and then riding around them until they lie down and fall asleep. Often, especially at first, this takes some time—the beasts will keep rising and lying down again. When at last most become quiet, some perverse brute of a steer will deliberately hook them all up; they keep moving in and out among one another, and long strings of animals suddenly start out from the herd at a stretching walk, and are turned back by the nearest cowboy only to break forth at a new spot. When finally they have lain down and are chewing their cud or slumbering, the two night guards begin riding round them in opposite ways, calling or singing to them, as the sound of the human voice seems to have a tendency to quiet them.

TRAILING CATTLE

THE HERD AT NIGHT

A STAMPEDE

Anything may start them — the plunge of a horse, the sudden approach of a coyote, or the arrival of some outside steers or cows that have smelt them and come up. Every animal in the herd will be on its feet in an instant, as if by an electric shock, and off with a rush, horns and tail up. Then, no matter how rough the ground nor how pitchy black the night, the cowboys must ride for all there is in them and spare neither their own nor their horses' necks. Once stopped, they may break again. I have known six such stops and renewed stampedes to take place in one night, the cowboy staying with his ever-diminishing herd of steers until daybreak.

IN A STAMPEDE

CUTTING OUT A STEER

To do good work in cutting out from a herd, not only should the rider be a good horseman, but he should also have a skillful, thoroughly trained horse. A good cutting pony is not common, and is generally too valuable to be used anywhere but in the herd. When looking through the herd, it is necessary to move slowly; and when any animal is found it is taken to the outskirts at a walk, so as not to alarm the others. Once at the outside, however, the cowboy has to ride like lightning; for as soon as the beast finds itself separated from its companions it endeavors to break back among them, and a young, range-raised steer or heifer runs like a deer.

CUTTING OUT A STEER

OUR HAZARDOUS BUSINESS

The truth is, ours is a primitive industry, and we suffer the reverses as well as enjoy the successes only known to primitive peoples. We still live in an iron age that the old civilized world has long passed by. The men of the border reckon upon stern and unending struggles with their iron-bound surroundings; against the grim harshness of their existence they set the strength and the abounding vitality that come with it. They run risks to life and limb that are unknown to the dwellers in cities; and what the men freely brave, the beasts that they own must also sometimes suffer.

AN EPISODE IN THE OPENING UP OF A CATTLE COUNTRY

CUSTER'S LAST BATTLE

E. S. Godfrey
Captain, 7th Cavalry

ON THE MARCH — THE ADVANCE GUARD

The 7th Cavalry was divided into two columns, designated the right and left wings, commanded by Major Marcus A. Reno and Captain F. W. Benteen. Each wing was subdivided into two battalions of three troops each. After the first day in the field, this was the habitual order of march: one battalion was advance-guard, one was rear-guard, and one marched on each flank of the train. General Custer, with one troop of the advance-guard, went ahead and selected the route for the train and the camping-places at the end of the day's march.

ON THE MARCH — THE ADVANCE GUARD

INDIAN SIGN

On the 19th of June tidings came from Reno that he had found a large trail that led up the Rosebud River. The particulars were not generally known. The camp was full of rumors; credulity was raised to the highest pitch, and we were filled with anxiety and curiosity until we reached Reno's command, and learned the details of their discoveries. They had found a large trail on the Tongue River, and had followed it up the Rosebud about forty miles. The number of lodges in the deserted villages was estimated by the number of camp-fires remaining to be about three hundred and fifty. The indications were that the trail was about three weeks old. No Indians had been seen, nor any recent signs. It is not probable that Reno's movements were known to the Indians, for on the very day Reno reached his farthest point up the Rosebud, the battle of the Rosebud, between General Crook's forces and the Indians, was fought. The two commands were then not more than forty miles apart, but neither knew nor even suspected the proximity of the other.

We reached the mouth of the Rosebud about noon on the 21st, and began preparations for the march and the battle of the Little Big Horn.

Upon assembling, General Custer gave us our orders. As soon as it was determined that we were to go out, nearly everyone took time to write letters home, but I doubt very much if there were many of a cheerful nature. Some officers made their wills, others gave verbal instructions as to the disposition of personal property and distribution of mementos. They seemed to have a presentiment of their fate.

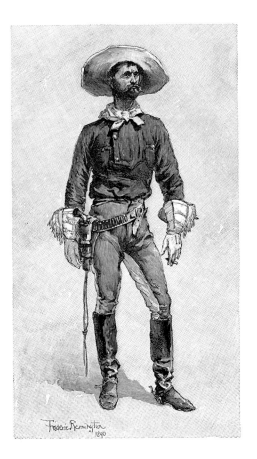

COURIERS

CAVALRY OFFICER IN CAMPAIGN DRESS

THE FRONTIER TROOPER'S THANATOPSIS

About sunset officers' call was sounded, and we assembled in General Custer's bivouac and squatted in groups about the General's bed. It was not a cheerful assemblage. Everyone seemed to be in a serious mood, and the small amount of conversation carried on before all had arrived was in undertones.

This "talk" of his, as we called it, was considered at the time something extraordinary for General Custer, for it was not his habit to unbosom himself to his officers. In it he showed a lack of self-confidence and a reliance on somebody else; there was an indefinable something that was not Custer. His manner and tone, usually brusque and aggressive, was on this occasion conciliating and subdued. There was something akin to an appeal that made a deep impression on all present.

After the meeting, Lieutenants McIntosh, Wallace, and myself walked to our bivouac, for some distance in silence, when Wallace remarked: "Godfrey, I believe General Custer is going to be killed." "Why, Wallace," I replied, "what makes you think so?" "Because," said he, "I have never heard Custer talk in that way before."

THE FRONTIER TROOPER'S THANATOPSIS

IN THE SCOUT BIVOUAC

I went to my troop and gave orders as to details for the morning preparations; I also gave directions in case of a night attack. I then went through the herd to satisfy myself as to the security of the horses. During the performance of this duty I came to the bivouac of the Indian scouts. I observed them for a few minutes, when one of them turned to me and said, "Have you ever fought against the Sioux?" "Yes," I replied. Then he asked, "Well, how many do you expect to find?" I answered, "It is said that we may find between one thousand and fifteen hundred." "Well, do you think we can whip that many?" "Oh, yes, I guess so," I replied. After he had interpreted our conversation, he said to me with a good deal of emphasis, "Well, I can tell you we are going to have a damn big fight!"

A FRIENDLY SCOUT SIGNALLING THE MAIN COLUMN

THE FLAG THAT FELL

On June 24th we passed a great many camping-places, all appearing to be of nearly the same strength. One would naturally suppose these were the successive camping-places of the same village, when in fact they were the campsites of the several bands. The fact that they appeared to have been made at the same time did not impress us then. Later we passed through one much larger than any of the others. The grass for a considerable distance around it had been cropped close, indicating that large herds had been grazed there.

At this time a stiff southerly breeze was blowing; as we were about to separate, the General's headquarter's flag was blown down, falling toward our rear. Being near the flag, I picked it up and stuck the staff in the ground, but it fell again to the rear. This circumstance made no impression on me at the time, but after the battle an officer asked me if I remembered the incident. He had observed it, and regarded the fact of its falling to the rear as a bad omen, and felt sure we would suffer a defeat.

SIGNALLING THE MAIN COMMAND

FOLLOWING A TRAIL

The march during the day was tedious. We made many long halts so as not to get ahead of the scouts, who seemed to be doing their work thoroughly. Once or twice, signal smokes were reported. The weather was dry and had been for some time, and consequently the trail was very dusty. The troopers were required to march on separate trails so that the dust clouds would not rise so high. The valley was heavily marked with lodge-pole trails and pony tracks, showing that immense herds of ponies had been driven over it.

"BOOTS AND SADDLES"

Sometime before eight o'clock, General Custer rode bareback to the several troops, gave orders to be ready to march at eight o'clock, and passed the information that scouts had discovered the locality of the Indian villages and camps in the valley of the Little Big Horn, about twelve or fifteen miles beyond the divide. Just before setting out on the march I went to where General Custer's bivouac was. The General, Bloody Knife, several Ree scouts, and a half-breed interpreter were squatted in a circle having a talk in the Indian fashion. The General wore a serious expression and was apparently abstracted. The scouts were doing the talking, and seemed nervous and disturbed. Finally, Bloody Knife made a remark that recalled the General from his reverie, and he asked in his usual quick, brusque manner, "What's that he says?" The interpreter replied, "He says that we'll find enough Sioux to keep us fighting two or three days." The General smiled and remarked, "I guess we'll get through with them in one day."

"BOOTS AND SADDLES"

FOLLOWING A TRAIL

SIZING THE OTHER UP

It is a rare occurrence in Indian warfare that gives a commander the opportunity to reconnoiter the enemy's position in daylight. This is particularly true if the Indians have a knowledge of the presence of troops in the country. When the signs indicate a hot trail, the commander judges his distance, and by a forced march in the night-time, tries to reach the Indian village at night and makes his disposition for a surprise attack at daylight. At all events his attack must be made with celerity, and generally without any other knowledge of the numbers of the opposing force save that discovered or conjectured while following the trail. If the advance to the attack be made in daylight, it is next to impossible that a near approach can be made without discovery.

It was well known to the Indians that the troops were in the field, and a battle was fully expected by them, but the close proximity of our column was not known to them until the morning of the day of the battle. Several young men had left the hostile camp on that morning to go to one of the agencies in Nebraska. They saw the dust made by the column of troops, and some of their number returned to the village and gave warning that the troops were coming. The attack was not a surprise.

A RECONNAISSANCE

INDIAN SCOUTS WATCHING CUSTER'S ADVANCE

RENO RETREATS

Reno, not seeing the "whole outfit" within supporting distance, did not obey his orders to charge the village, but dismounted his command to fight on foot. One man was killed close to where Reno was, and directly afterwards Reno gave orders to those near him to "mount and get to the bluffs." This order was not generally heard or communicated. While those who did hear it were preparing to execute it, he countermanded the order, but soon afterwards repeated it again.

Reno was with the foremost in this retreat — a "charge," as he later termed it in his report.

A number of officers collected on the edge of the bluff overlooking the valley and were discussing the situation; one of them remarked quite emphatically: "Gentlemen, in my opinion General Custer has made the biggest mistake of his life by not taking the whole regiment in at once in the first attack!" But no one seemed to show great anxiety, for everyone felt that Custer could and would take care of himself.

Some of Reno's men had seen a party of Custer's commmand, including Custer himself, on the bluffs about the time the Indians began to develop on Reno's front. It is possible, even probable, that from that high point Custer could then see nearly the whole camp and force of Indians and realized that the chances were desperate, but it was too late to reunite his forces for the attack. Reno was already in the fight and Custer's own battalion was separated from the attack by a distance of two and a half to three miles. He had no reason to think that Reno would not push his attack vigorously. A commander seldom goes into battle counting upon the failure of his subordinate; if he did, he certainly would provide that such failure should not turn into disaster.

MAJOR-GENERAL GEORGE A. CUSTER
from a photograph by Brady

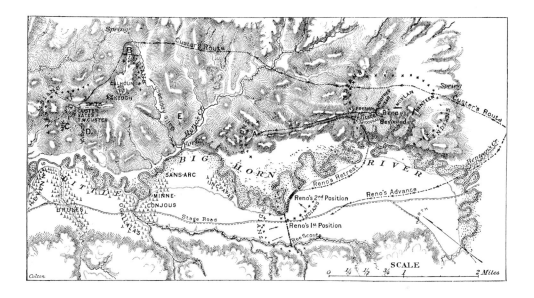

MAP OF CUSTER'S LAST BATTLE

A. Hill where Custer was seen by some of Reno's men during the fight in the valley; also the point reached by Reno's advance after the retreat from the valley, from which he fell back to the position in which he was besieged. B. Here Keogh's and Calhoun's troops dismounted and advanced along the ridge to where the bodies of their commands were found. C. A few bodies from the commands of Yates and T. W. Custer, who for the greater part died with Custer on the hill above, now known as Custer's Hill, and on which stands the monument shown on page 106. D. Ravine where were found bodies of many of Smith's troop who had formed in line on the ridge between Custer's and Keogh's position; Lieutenant Smith's body was found on Custer's Hill. E. Hill where Sergeant Butler's body was found; empty cartridge-shells lay about him. He belonged to Captain Custer's troop, and may have been carrying a message to Reno.

DISMOUNTED — MOVING THE LED HORSES

The line occupied by Custer's battalion was the first ridge back from the river, the nearest point being about half a mile from it. His front extended about three fourths of a mile. The whole village was in full view. A few hundred yards from his line was another but lower ridge, the further slope of which was not commanded by his line. It was here that the Indians under Crazy Horse formed for the charge on Custer's Hill. Gall collected his warriors, and moved up a ravine south of Keogh and Calhoun. As they were turning this flank, they discovered the led horses without any other guard than the horse-holders. They opened fire on the horse-holders, and used the usual devices to stampede the horses — yelling and waving blankets. In this they succeeded very soon, and the horses were caught up by the squaws. In this disaster Keogh and Calhoun probably lost their reserve ammunition, which was carried in the saddle-bags.

DISMOUNTED—THE FOURTH TROOPERS MOVING THE LED HORSES

OVERWHELMED

At a signal from Gall, the dismounted warriors rose and fired, and every Indian gave the war-whoop. The mounted Indians put whip to their ponies, and the whole mass rushed upon and crushed Calhoun. The maddened mass of Indians was carried forward by its own momentum over Calhoun and Crittenden down the depression where Keogh was with over thirty men, and all was over on that part of the field.

In the meantime, the same tactics were being pursued and executed around Custer's Hill. The warriors, under the leadership of Crow-King, Crazy Horse, White Bull, Hump, and others, moved up the ravine west of Custer's Hill, and concentrated under the shelter of the ridges on his right flank and back of his position. Gall's bloody work was finished before the annihilation of Custer was accomplished, so his victorious warriors hurried forward to the hot encounter then going on, and the frightful massacre was completed.

UNHORSED

AFTER THE BATTLE

Tuesday morning, June 27, we had reveille, enjoyed the pleasure of a square meal, and had our stock properly cared for. Our commanding officer seemed to think the Indians had some trap set for us, and required our men to hold themselves in readiness to occupy the rifle pits at a moment's notice.

About 9:30 A.M. a cloud of dust was observed several miles down the river. An hour of suspense followed, but from the slow advance we concluded that they were our troops. A soldier soon came up with a note from General Terry, addressed to General Custer, stating that two of our Crow scouts had been given information that our column had been whipped and nearly all had been killed. He did not believe their story, but was coming with medical assistance. Very soon after this, Lieutenant Bradley came into our lines, and asked where I was. Greeting my old friend most cordially, I immediately asked, "Where is Custer?" He replied, "I don't know, but I suppose he was killed, as we counted 197 dead bodies. I don't suppose any escaped." We were simply dumbfounded. This was the first intimation we had of his fate. It was hard to realize. It seemed impossible.

During the rest of that day we were busy collecting our effects and destroying surplus property. The wounded were cared for and taken to the camp of our new friends of the Montana column. On the morning of the 28th we left our entrenchments to bury the dead of Custer's command. The morning was bright, and from the high bluffs we had a clear view of Custer's battle-field. We saw a large number of objects that looked like white boulders scattered over the field. Field glasses were brought out, and soon it was announced that these objects were the dead bodies. Captain Weir exclaimed, "Oh, how white they look!"

WOUNDED SOLDIERS ON AN ESCORT WAGON

TAPS

All the bodies, except a few, were stripped of their clothing. According to my recollection nearly all were scalped or mutilated, but there was one notable exception, that of General Custer, whose face and expression were natural. He had been shot in the temple and in the left side. We buried, according to my memoranda, 212 bodies. The killed of the entire command was 265, and of wounded we had 52.

There were three main causes of Custer's defeat. The first concerns the overpowering numbers of the enemy and their unexpected cohesion. It seems incredible that such great numbers of Indians should have left the agencies to combine against the troops, and that no information of this sort was communicated to the commanders in the field. Reno's panic rout from the valley was the second cause. The Indians say that if Reno's position in the valley had been held, they would have been compelled to divide their strength for the different attacks, which would have caused confusion and apprehension, and would have prevented the concentration of every able-bodied warrior on Custer's battalion. The third cause was the defective extraction of empty cartridge-shells from the carbines. When cartridges were dirty or corroded the ejectors did not always extract the empty shells from the chambers, and the men were compelled to use knives to get them out. When shells were clean, no difficulty was experienced.

A battle was unavoidable. Every man in Terry's and Custer's commands expected a battle; it was for that purpose, to punish the Indians, that the command was sent out, and with that determination Custer made his preparations. Had Custer continued his march southward — that is, left the Indian trail — the Indians would have known of our movement on the 25th, and a battle would have been fought very near the same place where Crook had been attacked and forced back a week before. The Indians would have never remained in camp and allowed a concentration of several columns of troops to attack them. If they had escaped without punishment or battle, Custer undoubtedly would have been blamed.

"TAPS" (CAVALRY OFFICER IN FULL UNIFORM)

SHERIFF'S WORK ON A RANCH

Theodore Roosevelt

MAKING THE CAPTURE

The three men we suspected of stealing our boat had long been accused — justly or unjustly — of being implicated both in cattle-killing and in that worst of frontier crimes, horse-stealing: it was only by accident that they had escaped the clutches of the vigilantes the preceding fall. Their leader was a well-built fellow named Finnigan, who had long hair reaching to his shoulders, and always wore a broad hat and a fringed buckskin shirt. He was rather a hard case, and had been chief actor in a number of shooting scrapes. The other two were a stout, muscular man and an old German, whose viciousness was of the weak and shiftless type.

We knew that these three men were becoming uneasy and were anxious to leave the locality; and we also knew that traveling on horseback, in the direction in which they would wish to go, was almost impossible, as the swollen, ice-fringed rivers could not be crossed at all, and the stretches of broken ground would form nearly impassable barriers. The men we were after knew that they had taken with them the only craft there was on the river, and so felt perfectly secure; accordingly, we took them absolutely by surprise. Their camp was under the lee of a cut bank, behind which we crouched, and, after waiting over an hour, they came in.

When they were within twenty yards or so we straightened up from behind the bank, covering them with our cocked rifles, while I shouted to them to hold up their hands. Finnigan hesitated for a second, his eyes fairly wolfish; then, as I walked up within a few paces, covering the center of his chest to avoid overshooting, and repeating the command, he saw he had no show, and, with an oath, let his rifle drop and held his hands up beside his head.

"HANDS UP!" — THE CAPTURE OF FINNIGAN

ONE OF THE BOYS

ON GUARD

It was nearly dusk, so we camped where we were. The first thing to be done was to collect enough wood to enable us to keep a blazing fire all night long. Having captured our men, we were in a quandary how to keep them. The cold was so intense that to tie them tightly hand and foot meant, in all likelihood, freezing both hands and feet off during the night; and it was no use tying them at all unless we tied them tightly enough to stop in part the circulation. So nothing was left for us to do but keep perpetual guard over them. By this time they were pretty well cowed, as they found out very quickly that they would be well treated so long as they remained quiet, but would receive some pretty rough handling if they attempted any disturbance.

"TAKE OFF YOUR BOOTS!"

Immediately afterward we made the men take off their boots — an additional safeguard, as it was a cactus country, in which a man could travel barefoot only at the risk of laming himself for life — and go to bed, all three lying on one buffalo robe and being covered by another, in the full light of the blazing fire. For this night-watching we always used the double-barrel with buckshot, as a rifle is uncertain in the dark; while with a shot-gun at such a distance, and with men lying down, a person who is watchful may be sure that they cannot get up, no matter how quick they are, without being riddled.

ON GUARD AT NIGHT

"TAKE OFF YOUR BOOTS!"

DOWN-STREAM

We broke camp in the morning, on a point of land covered with brown, leafless, frozen cottonwoods; and in the afternoon we pitched camp on another point in the midst of a grove of the same stiff, dreary trees. The discolored river, whose eddies boiled into yellow foam, flowed always between the same banks of frozen mud or of muddy ice. And what was, from our standpoint, even worse, our diet began to be as same as the scenery. Being able to kill nothing, we exhausted all our stock of provisions and got reduced to flour, without yeast or baking-powder; and unleavened bread, made with exceedingly muddy water, is not, as a steady thing, attractive.

DOWN-STREAM

BORROWING THE WAGON

But when the day was darkest the dawn appeared. At last, having worked down some thirty miles at the tail of the ice jam, we struck an outlying cow-camp of the C Diamond (C◇) ranch, and knew that our troubles were almost over. There was but one cowboy in it, but we were certain of his cordial help, for in a stock country all make common cause against either horse-thieves or cattle-thieves. He had no wagon, but told us we could get one at a nearby ranch, and lent me a pony to go up there and see about it, which I accordingly did, after a sharp preliminary tussle when I came to mount the wiry bronco. When I reached the ranch, I was able to hire a large prairie schooner and two tough little bronco mares. The settler, a rugged old plainsman, could hardly understand why I took so much bother with the thieves instead of hanging them off-hand.

"A SHARP PRELIMINARY TUSSLE"

ON THE ROAD TO DICKINSON

Soon we were able to take the three thieves in to Dickinson, the nearest town. The going was bad, and the little mares could only drag the wagon at a walk, so, though we drove during the daylight, it took us two days and a night to make the journey. It was a most desolate drive. The prairie had been burned the fall before, and was a mere bleak waste of blackened earth, and a cold, rainy mist lasted throughout the two days. At night, when we put up in the squalid hut of a frontier granger, the only habitation on our road, it was even worse. I did not dare to go to sleep, but making my three men get into the upper bunk, I sat up with my back against the cabin door and kept watch over them all night long. So, after thirty-six hours of sleeplessness, I was most heartily glad when we at last jolted into the long, straggling main street of Dickinson, and I was able to give my unwilling companions into the hands of the sheriff.

ON THE ROAD TO DICKINSON

THE NORTHWEST MOUNTED POLICE OF CANADA

J. G. A. Creighton

THE FIRST EXPEDITION

In 1873 the Dominion of Canada had a serious problem to face. It had bought Rupert's Land from the Hudson Bay Company four years previously. Since all beyond the Red River was practically unknown, an army of regular troops seemed necessary to take and keep possession. The nucleus of the force was got together in Manitoba, in the autumn of 1873, and the rest, making the strength only three hundred in all, went from Toronto to Fargo by rail in June of 1874 and then marched 160 miles to Dufferin, on the southern frontier of Manitoba. With two field-guns and two mortars, and relying on their own transport train for supplies, they then marched 800 miles westward through an unknown country inhabited by 30,000 Indians and a few score white desperadoes until the Rocky Mountains were in sight. Leaving one detachment to build a fort in the very heart of the country of the terrible Blackfeet, where no white man's life was then safe, and sending another detachment north to Edmonton among the Assiniboines and Wood Crees, the main column turned back. They crossed the plains northward by way of Qu'Appelle to Fort Pelly, but finding their intended headquarters were not ready they returned to Dufferin. The thermometer, which had stood at 100° F. in the shade when they marched out, marked 30° below zero on their return. In four months, to a day, they travelled 1,959 miles, besides the distances covered by detachments on special service.

Many good horses lived through want of water and food on the arid plains only to die from the effects of unaccustomed forage, or from the bitter cold that came on early in the autumn, though officers and men gave up their blankets to shelter their charges. But the three hundred Police accomplished, without losing a life, what had seemed work for an army — the taking possession of the Great Lone Land.

ONE OF THE RIDERS

CLEANING OUT THE GREAT LONE LAND

One object of that first expedition was to drive out the gangs of whiskey traders, outlaws of the worst kind from the Western States, who kept the Indians in a chronic state of deviltry, and only the year before had committed a number of murders and outrages on their own account. The forts in which they were reported to be entrenched proved to be merely trading posts, built of logs, and the inmates had taken themselves off without giving the police a chance to fire a shot. Another object was to establish friendly relations with the Indians. This was soon accomplished, and their confidence in the police has lasted from that day to this. Their suspicions quickly wore away, and they became outspoken in their expressions of gratitude to the Government for sending them such protectors. As one chief told Colonel Macleod, "Before you came the Indian crept along, now he is not afraid to walk erect."

A SERIOUS WARNING

IN THE FACE OF DANGER

In 1877 nearly the whole of the little force was concentrated on the southwestern frontier to watch and check the 6,000 Sioux who sought refuge in Canada after their defeat of Custer on the Little Big Horn. A time of great anxiety ensued. The Canadian Indians, especially the Blackfeet, were strongly opposed to the presence of the Sioux — the more so as it was already apparent that the buffalo would be extinct in a few years. The temptation was great to smoke the tobacco sent them by the Sioux runners, and thus bind themselves to join in an effort to sweep out once and for all the white men, whose numbers seemed so scanty. But — chiefly under Crowfoot's influence — it was resisted, and they helped the Police by refraining from hostilities, and affording information as to the doings of the new-comers. Sitting Bull and his warriors were met with a quiet resolution that astonished them, and won their immediate respect. They were told that so long as they observed the law they would be protected, but could expect nothing more, and would not be allowed to settle permanently in Canada. They were finally induced to surrender peacefully to the United States authorities in 1880-81.

The coolness and pluck of the Police during that critical period were amazing. Their confidence in themselves is curiously evidenced by a report from the officer in command at Wood Mountain, recommending that at least 50 men should be stationed there, as there were about 5,000 Sioux camped in the vicinity!

THE CANADIAN MOUNTED POLICE ON A "MUSICAL RIDE" — "CHARGE!"

TRADITIONS AND DUTIES

Though organized when the late Hon. Alexander Mackenzie was Premier, the Mounted Police were one of Sir John Macdonald's inspirations, and after his return to power in 1878, they always remained under his own eye. The red coat was no mere concession to historic sentiment, but his crafty appeal to Indian tradition of the good faith and fighting qualities of the "King George's Man" whose ally the brethren in the East had been, and to whom even the great Hudson Bay Company owed allegiance.

The Northwest Mounted Police, like the Royal Irish Constabulary, on which it was modelled, is, in the eye of the law, a purely civil body; its officers are magistrates, the men are constables. But so far as circumstances will allow, its organization, internal economy, and drill are those of a cavalry regiment, and when on active service in a military capacity, the officers have army rank.

The statutory duty of the Mounted Police is to carry out the criminal and other laws of the Dominion in the Northwest Territories, and, if required to do so, in every province of Canada. There is hardly anything that they have not to turn their hands to in the myriad circumstances of the vast country through which they are scattered.

A MOUNTED POLICEMAN

A COMMENDATION

"I have asked for this parade this morning . . . to express my entire satisfaction at the manner in which your duties have been performed. You have been subjected to some searching criticism, for on my staff are officers who have served in the cavalry, artillery, and infantry. Their unanimous verdict is to the effect that they have never seen work better, more willingly, or more smartly done while under circumstances of some difficulty caused by bad weather or otherwise . . . Your force is often spoken of in Canada as one of which Canada is justly proud. It is well that this pride is so fully justified, for your duties are most important and varied. The perfect confidence in the maintenance of the authority of the law prevailing over these vast territories, a confidence most necessary with the settlement now proceeding, shows how thoroughly you have done your work . . ."

— Lord Lorne, Governor-General of Canada

OFFICER OF THE MOUNTED POLICE IN FULL DRESS

SOME AMERICAN RIDERS

Colonel Theodore Ayrault Dodge, U.S.A.

A PLAINS INDIAN

The bareback rider was common among the Plains Indians of forty years ago. A piece of buffalo-robe girthed over the pony's back stood in lieu of saddle, if even so much was used; a cord of twisted hair lashed round its lower jaw served for bit and bridle. His bow and arrows gave full occupation to his hands: he had to guide his pony with legs and word alone, and relied on its intelligence and the training he had given it to do the right thing at the right time. Thus slenderly equipped, this superb rider dashed into the midst of a herd of buffalo, and so quick was the pony and so strong the seat of his master that, despite the stampede of the terror-stricken herd and the charges of the enraged and wounded bulls, few accidents ever occurred. The Indian on horseback has ninety lives, not nine. His riding is not an art, it is nature.

AN OLD-TIME NORTHERN PLAINS INDIAN — THE COUP

A WHITE TRAPPER

The white trapper was as averse to association with his fellow man as the hardiest of the old pioneers. In fact he often fled the settlements for good and sufficient cause. He has now all but died out, with the buffalo, though a generation ago he was a common enough character in the territories north of Colorado. His sons have turned cowpunchers.

This famous hunter was a character more practical than poetic, though he has been made the subject of many fine phrases and the hero of many exaggerated situations. His hair and beard floated long and loose under his coyote cap, and he had lived so continuously with the Indians that he had largely adopted their dress and manners, could if need be live on the same chuck, and always had one or more squaws. He rode a Mexican saddle, for which he had traded skins — or perhaps had stolen — and from which he had cut every strip of superfluous leather, as the Indian does today. He rode the same pony as his Indian competitor in the trade, but with a seat adapted to a saddle rather than a pad, and still retaining a flavor of the settlements despite his divorce from their ways.

A WHITE TRAPPER

AN INDIAN TRAPPER

The Indian trapper whom our artist has depicted may be a Cree, or perhaps a Blackfoot, whom one was apt to run across in the Selkirk Mountains or elsewhere on the plains of the British Territory, or well up north in the Rockies, toward the outbreak of the Civil War. He rode a pony which had nothing to distinguish him from the Plains pony, except that in winter his coat grew to so remarkable a length as to almost conceal the identity of the animal. Unless you saw it in motion, you might take it for a huge species of bear with a tail.

This trapper rode a pad, which was not unlike an air-cushion, cinched in place and provided with a pair of very short stirrups hung exactly from the middle. This dragged the heels to the rear, in the fashion of the old-time Sioux, and gave him a very awkward seat. By just what process, from a bareback seat, the fellow managed to drift into this one, which is quite peculiar to himself, is hard to guess.

AN INDIAN TRAPPER

THE TRAVAUX PONY

As the patient ass to the follower of the Prophet, so is the travaux pony to the Indian. It is hard to say which bears the most load according to his capacity, the donkey or the pony. Either earns what he gets with fourfold more right than his master. The travaux pony furnishes the sole means of transportation of the Indian camp, and, weight for weight, drags on his tepee poles more than the best mule in Uncle Sam's service does on an Army wagon. When camp is broken, the squaws strip the tent-poles of their buffalo-skin coverings, and it is these poles which furnish the wheels of the Indian vehicle. Thus laden, the wonderful little beast, which is rarely up to fourteen hands, plods along all day, covering unheard-of distances, and living on bunch-grass, with a mouthful of water now and then.

THE TRAVAUX PONY

A MODERN COMANCHE

The Comanche of the Fort Sill region is a good type of the Indian of today. He is the most expert horse-stealer on the Plains if we can credit the Indians themselves, who yield to him the palm as a sneak-thief — with them a title of honor rather than of reproach. There is no boldness or dash in his method, but he is all the more dangerous. The Comanche is fond of gay clothes, and has a trick of wrapping a sheet around his body, doubling in the ends, and letting the rest fall about his legs. This gives him the look of wearing the skirts or leg-gear of the Oriental.

In one particular the Comanche is noteworthy. He knows more about a horse and horse-breeding than any other Indian. He is particularly wedded to and apt to ride a pinto ("painted" or piebald) horse, and never keeps any but a pinto stallion. He chooses his ponies well, and shows more good sense in breeding than one would give him credit for. The corollary to this is that the Comanche is far less cruel to his beasts, and though he begins to use them as yearlings, the ponies often last through many years. The Comanche is capable of making as fine cavalry as exists if subjected to discipline and carefully drilled.

MODERN COMANCHE

AN APACHE INDIAN

The Apache of the present day lives in the Sierra Madre in Arizona. He is not born and bred with horses, he knows little about them, and looks upon ponies as intended quite as much for food as for transportation or the war-path. He will eat all his ponies during the winter, and rely upon stealing fresh ones in the spring: he and the Cheyenne are the most dashing of the horse-thieves. He raids down in Chihuahua where the vaqueros raise stock for the Mexican army, and often drives off large numbers. When pursued, the Apache takes to the mountains, and is sometimes compelled to abandon his herd. He steals his saddles in Mexico, wears spurs when he can get them to drive his pony, and if these do not suffice to make him go his gait, will goad him with a knife. In the mountains, where the sharp, flinty stones soon wear down the pony's unshod feet, this Indian will shrink rawhide over the hoofs in lieu of shoes, and this resists extremely well the attrition of the mountain paths. Arrian tells us that the Macedonians, under Alexander, did the same to their cavalry horses in the Caucasus, and no doubt the habit was much older than Alexander.

AN APACHE INDIAN

A UNITED STATES CAVALRYMAN

Considering all the circumstances — that the cavalry recruit is often a city-bred lad, who knows practically nothing about a horse, and has to be taught it all; that he is employed too much on duties which unfit him for his work; that he as well as his horse has to be acclimated; and that the whole business which is new to him is an old story to the Indian — it is astonishing how well he does. His performances reflect unlimited credit upon his superiors.

Let us look at some good distance riding, for it is in this that our men excel. General Merritt in 1879 rode with a battalion of the Fifth Cavalry to the relief of Payne, and covered one hundred and seventy miles from 11 A.M., October 2nd, to 5:30 P.M., October 5th — two days and six hours — accompanied by a battalion of infantry in wagons, which much retarded the march. He arrived on the scene in good order and ready for a fight. Captain F. S. Dodge marched his command on the same occasion eighty miles in sixteen hours. Lieutenant Wood, of the Fourth Cavalry, marched his troop seventy miles in twelve hours — 6 A.M. to 6 P.M. — and came in fresh; and double that distance has been made from 10 A.M. till 5 P.M. next day. These are but a few out of scores of equal performances. Men who can do work like this and come in fresh must be consummate horsemen.

UNITED STATES CAVALRYMAN

THE INDIAN SCOUT

In constant association with the cavalryman is the Indian scout. There are two hundred and seventy-five of these men enlisted in the army, and many more have been temporarily in service. The enlisted ones receive the pay and allowances of the cavalry soldier. They come of all tribes. The Indian scout finds his own ponies, but has issued to him a government saddle and equipments, and barring spurs, for which he substitutes the invariable quirt, delights in Uncle Sam's uniform. We are indebted to him for much of the best service, and in his ranks have been numbered many men whose names are household words.

INDIAN SCOUT WITH LOST TROOP HORSE

CANADIAN MOUNTED POLICE

The Canadian Mounted Police is an uncommonly fine body of men, numbering on its roster many of the better classes. They have the usual military organization, but are distributed in small groups all over Canada. Their duties are chiefly to suppress the whiskey trade — for fire-water is still the greatest of the Indian's foes — keep the Indians in subjection, and aid the sheriffs of the various counties. These men ride a bred-up bronco, and their saddle is what is known as the Montana tree. The Canadian Mounted Police is one of the most efficient organizations which exists; and it accomplishes its purpose because it is not interfered with. Its work tells and is appreciated, as the much harder and more dangerous duties of our cavalry are not.

A COWBOY

The cowboy is in the saddle more than any man on the Plains. He is careful of his ponies, not only from a horseman's motives, but because he is held to account for them. The cowboy's bit is any kind of curb with a long gag. He rides under all conditions with a loose rein, the bit ends of which are of chain, which clanks a rhythmic jingle to his easy lope. His pony is as surefooted as a mountain goat, and will safely scramble with his big load up a cliff, or slide down a bank which would make our tenderfoot hair stand on end.

The most striking part of a cowboy's rig is the chaperajos, or huge leathern overalls, he is apt to wear. These originated in the mesquite or chaparral country, where the cattle business had its origin, and where jeans or a pair of the best cords will be torn to shreds in a day. The cowboy is unequalled in his own province, and this is enough of fame. It is a common feat for him to put a playing-card on the saddle, or a dollar piece under each foot in the stirrup, or under his knees, and ride a vigorous bucker.

CANADIAN MOUNTED POLICE

COWBOY LIGHTING THE RANGE FIRE

TEACHING A MUSTANG PONY TO PACK DEAD GAME

There is no creature in the service of man which can put his master to such violent efforts in his subjugation as the bronco. Of course a better plan would be the more gradual one of civilized trainers, but for this there is no time.

TEACHING A MUSTANG PONY TO PACK DEAD GAME

"BREAKING"

The whole secret of "breaking" lies in completely exhausting the bronco at the first lesson; he will never buck "for keeps" more than once. But once ridden to the verge of falling in his tracks, the pony will not do his level worst again, but content himself with grunting and yelling, and playing the devil generally.

Breaking is a fair fight and no favor between man and beast. But the buster has been there before, and knows exactly what he is about; the bronco is new to the business, and though he invariably makes a good fight, he is sure to have to give in.

THE INDIAN METHOD OF BREAKING A PONY

A MEXICAN VAQUERO

The American cowboy has a Mexican cousin, the vaquero, who does cow-punching in Chihuahua, and raises horses for the Mexican cavalry and an occasional shipment across the Rio Grande. Our vaquero wears white cotton clothes, and goat-skin chaperajos with the hair left on, naked feet, and huarachos, or sandals, and big jingling spurs. A gourd, lashed to his cantle, does the duty of canteen. He is supposed to be a famous rider, and is a very good one. He breaks his own ponies, which sufficiently proves his case. The Mexican cow-ponies are traditionally tough and serviceable.

A GENTLEMAN RIDER

Our artist has drawn the typical rider on the Paseo de la Reforma in the city of Mexico. In this style ride both the statesman and the swell, the banker and (when he can afford it) his clerk. The first thing in our Mexican friend which strikes us is his horse. This is not the bronco of the plains. He is evidently imported from Spain, or lately bred from Spanish stock, without that long struggle for existence which has given the pony his wonderful endurance and robbed him of every mark of external beauty. Here we revert to the original Moorish type. The high and long-maned crest, arched with pride, the full red nostril, large and docile eye, rounded barrel, high croup, tail set on and carried to match the head, clean legs, high action, and perfect poise. How he fills our artistic eye! How we dwell upon him! But we must remember that performance comes first, beauty after, and that the meanest runt of a Plains pony, on a ride of a hundred miles across the Bad Lands, would leave this beautiful animal dead in his tracks full twoscore miles behind!

A MEXICAN VAQUERO

GENTLEMAN RIDER ON THE PASEO DE LA REFORMA

A SOUTHERN RIDER

When the Northern farmer goes to the nearest town he drives, because the roads are good, and he can carry his stuff to better advantage; the Southerner rides, because the roads for a great part of the year are impassable to wheels. This breeds the universal habit of horseback work. The Southerner has been in the saddle for many generations, and today boys and girls alike ride the colts in pasture, with only a stick to guide them.

The first duty of the cross-country rider is to save his horse, because the service required of him in each occasion of use is exceptionally great. The road-rider need not do this, because he covers but a tithe of the distance at any one time. Hence the rule of the road is that the horse shall, first of all, subserve his rider's comfort. The most comfort resides primarily in ease; next in variety of gaits. And no one who has learned the Southern gaits can deny their superior ease. The proof lies in the fact that they enable a man to ride without undue exertion in hot or cold weather. Nothing can be more inspiring than a fine open trot; but a horse which can go Southern gaits can trot besides, and if the rider is as clever as he, without injury to his other paces.

A SOUTHERN RIDER

A HUNTING MAN

In a few sections of the country, fox-hunting has become not only an hereditary sport, but also one in which the farmers take an equal part and interest. This is as it should be. Hunting can never thrive when only the rich can indulge in it. But it is probable that hunting has taken firm root: although the climate cannot be coaxed nor foxes quickly bred, there is small danger that the riding part of the sport will soon be lost.

A HUNTING MAN

FROM WORK TO SPORT

Sport has shown us what excellent material we have in this country for hunters. Our American horses have done better across our country than the expensive imported English and Irish ones. The difficulty of acclimation has something to do with this; but few things have shown the adaptability of our stock to any work better than the number of horses of trotting blood that have turned out fast gallopers, big timber-jumpers, and stayers.

RUNNING A COYOTE WITH HOUNDS IN SOUTHERN CALIFORNIA

POLO-PLAYERS

The American polo pony is none other than our bronco friend. Many come from Texas, Wyoming, and Montana. The clever cow-pony is ready trained for the polo ground. He will catch the idea of the game as quickly as he caught the trick of cow-punching, for he has already learned to stop and turn and twist as only he can do. It must not be forgotten that he has precisely the same blood in his veins which has placed the English thoroughbred so far above all other horses. He has increased his stock of endurance and hardiness by his struggle for existence on the Plains, and for this game he is perhaps the equal of any pony, whatever his breeding, and within the limits of the polo field his speed is just as great — and some judges say greater.

POLO-PLAYERS

JOCKEYS

How many modern jockeys study their horses, or can cut and whip a race out of a slug, or wheedle it out of a sulky jade? They use steel and whalebone on the willing and unwilling alike. Delicate mouth-touching is the rarest of the jockey's arts, and almost every jockey here "rides twice as quick as his horse is going."

There has as yet been no phenomenal jockey produced in America. But it may be fairly claimed that our best jockeys come well up in the second rank. That the common jockey here is less good than in England is simply due to the fact that there he serves at least a species of apprenticeship, while here he has none.

Copyright, 1890,
By
Frederic Remington

JOCKEYS

THE RANCHMAN'S RIFLE ON CRAG AND PRAIRIE

Theodore Roosevelt

GOING HUNTING

The ranchman owes to his rifle not only the keen pleasure and strong excitement of the chase, but also much of his bodily comfort; for, save for his prowess as a hunter and his skill as a marksman with this, his favorite weapon, he would almost always be stinted for fresh meat. Now that the buffalo have gone, and the Sharps rifle by which they were destroyed is also gone, almost all ranchmen use some form of repeater. Personally I prefer the Winchester, using the new model, with a 45-caliber bullet of 300 grains, backed by 90 grains of powder.

A small band of elk yet linger round a great patch of prairie and Bad Lands some thirty-five miles off. In 1885 I killed a good bull out of the lot; and once last season, when we were sorely in need of meat for smoking and drying, we went after them again. With much difficulty we got together a scrub wagon team of four as unkempt, dejected, and vicious-looking broncos as ever stuck fast in quicksand or balked in pulling up a steep pitch. Their driver was a crack whip, and their load light, consisting of little but the tent and bedding; but as the river was high and the horses were weak, we came within an ace of being swamped at one crossing, and the country was so very rough that we were only able to get the wagon up the worst pitch by hauling from the saddle with the riding-animals.

We camped by an excellent spring of cold, clear water — not a common luxury in the Bad Lands. The first day we spent in trying to find the probable locality of our game; and after beating pretty thoroughly over the smoother country, towards nightfall we found quite fresh elk tracks leading into a stretch of very rough and broken land about ten miles from camp.

Our outfit was simple, as we carried only blankets, a light wagon-sheet, the ever-present camera, flour, bacon, salt, sugar, and coffee; canned goods are very unhandy to pack about on horseback. Our rifles and ammunition, with the few cooking-utensils and a book or two, completed the list. Four solemn ponies and a ridiculous little mule named Walla Walla bore us and our belongings.

OUR CAMP

OUR ELK OUTFIT AT THE FORD

DOWN BRAKES!

IN A CANYON OF THE COEUR D'ALÈNE

Driving a pack train through the wooded paths and up the mountain passes that we had to traverse is hard work anyhow, as there are sure to be accidents happening to the animals all the time, while their packs receive rough treatment from jutting rocks and overhanging branches, or from the half-fallen tree-trunks under which the animals wriggle; and if the loads are continually coming loose, or slipping so as to gall the horses' backs and make them sore, the labor and anxiety are increased tenfold.

In a day or two we were in the heart of the vast wooded wilderness. A broad, lonely river ran through its midst, cleaving asunder the mountain chains. Range after range, peak upon peak, the mountains towered on every side, the lower timbered to the top, the higher with bare crests of gray crags or else hooded with fields of shining snow. Over the whole land lay like a shroud the mighty growth of the unbroken evergreen forest — spruce and hemlock, fir, balsam, tamarack, and lofty pine.

IN A CANYON OF THE COEUR D'ALÈNE

THE INDIANS WE MET

At first we did not have good weather. The Indians, of whom we met a small band — Flatheads or their kin, on a visit from the coast region — had set fire to the woods not far away, and the smoke became so dense as to hurt our eyes, to hide the sun at midday, and to veil all objects from our sight as completely as if there had been a heavy fog. Then we had two days of incessant rain, which rendered our camp none too comfortable; but when this cleared we found that it had put out the fire and settled all the smoke, leaving a brilliant sky overhead.

THE INDIANS WE MET

STALKING GOATS

White goats have been known to hunters ever since Lewis and Clark crossed the continent, but they have always ranked as the very rarest and most difficult to get of all American game. This reputation they owe to the nature of their haunts, rather than to their own wariness, for they have been so little disturbed that they are less shy than either deer or sheep. They are very conspicuous animals, with their snow-white coats and polished black horns, but their pursuit necessitates so much toil and hardship that not one in ten of the professional hunters has ever killed one; and I know of but one or two Eastern sportsmen who can boast a goat's head as a trophy.

THE FIRST SHOT

I had been, as usual, walking and clambering over the mountains all day long, and in mid-afternoon reached a great slide, with halfway across it a tree. Under this I sat down to rest, my back to the trunk, and had been there but a few minutes when my companion suddenly whispered to me that a goat was coming down the slide at its edge, near the woods. I was in a most uncomfortable position for a shot. I cautiously tried to shift my position, and at once dislodged some pebbles, at the sound of which the goat sprang promptly up on the bank, his whole mien changing into one of alert, alarmed curiosity. He was less than a hundred yards off, so I risked a shot, all cramped and twisted though I was. But my bullet went low, and he disappeared over the bank like a flash.

I suppose the sport to be had among the tremendous mountain masses of the Himalayas must stand above all other kinds of hill shooting; yet after all it is hard to believe that it can yield much more pleasure than that felt by the American hunter when he follows the lordly elk and the grizzly among the timbered slopes of the Rockies, or the big-horn and the white-fleeced, jet horned antelope goat over their towering and barren peaks.

STALKING GOATS

THE FIRST SHOT

BESIEGED BY THE UTES

THE MASSACRE OF 1879

E. V. Sumner
Lt. Colonel, 5th Cavalry

THE UTE AFFAIR

In the summer of 1879, trouble occurred between the White River Utes and their agent, N. C. Meeker. The cause is not important, but the trouble finally became serious enough to warrant the call upon the Secretary of War for the support of troops to repress turbulence and disorder among the Indians of that nation.

This Ute campaign was a repetition of all the other sad occurrences in Indian warfare. Major Thornburgh, the commander, as noble and brave a man as ever marched with troops, fell as others had, having ignored an enemy in the morning who had the power to defeat him before noon.

ON OUTPOST DUTY

UNDER SIEGE

Thornburgh, after leaving his infantry company at a supply camp, pushed on with his three troops of cavalry, and while on the march on the 29th of September, at 10 A.M., at the crossing of Milk River, the Indians opened fire on the column from all directions, and from what followed it would appear that the command was completely surprised, sufficiently so to make some confusion among the troops.

The loss of the animals and the number of wounded men to be cared for and protected made any movement from this spot out of the question. There was nothing to do then but fight it out and hold on until reinforcements could reach them. The first night was employed by the troops in building a breastwork near the water, and in caring for the wounded.

There being no timber within reach, shelter had to be constructed from such material as was at hand. The wagons were unloaded, and bundles of bedding, sacks of grain, cracker-boxes and bacon sides were piled up, and the bodies of dead horses and mules were dragged to the line and made use of for defense. A pit was sunk in the center of this square.

BEHIND THE BREASTWORK

SENDING FOR HELP

After dark on this first night a volunteer was called to take one of the horses yet left alive and if possible steal his way through the enemy's line to the nearest telegraph station. The volunteer for this desperate mission successfully accomplished the distance of 170 miles in less than 24 hours.

ARRIVAL OF A COURIER

CAPTAIN DODGE'S COLORED TROOPERS TO THE RESCUE

At an early hour on the morning of October 2nd, the sentinel heard the approach of a column of horsemen, and the besieged soon welcomed Captain Dodge, 9th Cavalry, at the head of his troop. The Captain, having heard of the situation, came at once to the assistance of his comrades, and managed to get through to the entrenchment without losing any of his men. This reinforcement of two officers and fifty enlisted men added materially to the fighting strength of his command, and they brought with them also the cheering news that the courier had passed through safely.

The gallant dash made by these colored troopers brought them into high favor with the rest of the command, and nothing was considered too good for the "Buffalo" soldiers after that.

CAPTAIN DODGE'S COLORED TROOPERS TO THE RESCUE

REINFORCEMENTS!

General Merritt at this time was some distance ahead with the cavalry, and crossing the last hill he entered the valley just at the dawn of day. It was yet too dark to see the entrenchment, but the column, while pressing on, was soon brought to a halt by a challenge from the besieged. A trumpeter was then summoned and officers' call sounded. This brought all hands to the top of the breastwork, and a lively cheer answered the last note of the trumpet.

A wild scene followed this coming together of old comrades, and while it was going on, the enemy, although at their posts within easy range, did not fire a shot. Nor did they seem to be alarmed by the arrival of this overpowering force, but were for the time being quiet spectators of this grand reunion, their portion of the fun probably being in the supposition of "more horses, more shoot him."

UTES WATCHING FOR THE RELIEF COLUMN

THE END OF THE SIEGE

The rear was safe in the hands of the infantry, and the cavalry was ordered to take the nearest hills on the flanks. This accomplished, the General moved out a short distance to the front, having a troop of cavalry as escort, but did not advance half a mile before being fired upon.

Under existing circumstances, an enemy would have made a hasty retreat over the mountains, and any strategist in command could have made certain calculations, but these Ute Indians, instinctively brave and not at all instructed, had the utmost confidence in their power to resist any number of soldiers attacking them in their mountain homes.

In this short campaign there were 13 men killed and 48 wounded, out of a command of 150 strong. The papers throughout the country mentioned it for a day or two as "the Ute Affair," and there it rests, being one of several tragic instances where the percentage of loss is greater than that experienced in battles to which monuments are being erected and elaborate memorials published to commemorate deeds of bravery.

INFANTRY COVERING THE WITHDRAWAL OF CAVALRY

A TERRIBLE SIGHT

After the command brought down by General Merritt had been well rested and was ready for another advance, it proceeded through the mountains to White River and the agency. No attack would have been made on that column without due warning, and the result was that we crossed the high hills and wound through canyon after canyon, reaching the valley of the White River and the agency without hearing a shot or, to my knowledge, seeing an Indian.

At the agency a horrible sight presented itself. Every building had been burned, the bodies of all the male employees were stretched upon the ground where they had been murdered a few days before, and the women had been carried off into a captivity worse than death.

CROW INDIANS FIRING INTO THE AGENCY

ANOTHER TRAGEDY

We had still another sad experience, and a reminder that the Utes were still near us and relentless enough to take any advantage presenting itself.

A party under Lieutenant Hall, regimental quartermaster, was sent out to reconnoiter and look for a trail across the mountains from White River to Grand River. With this party was Lieutenant William Bayard Weir, and his sergeant, Humme. Weir was out as a volunteer to accompany Hall, and to hunt. As the party was riding along the trail, a small herd of deer was discovered off to the left in a ravine. Weir and Humme went after them, while Hall kept on to the front. He had not gone far, however, before he saw fresh Indian signs, and soon afterwards heard sharp firing to his left and rear. On turning back to ascertain the cause and to help Weir should he be in trouble, he was fired upon himself, and discovered that he was surrounded by Indians. He covered his party as quickly as possible in the dry bed of a stream near at hand, and kept the Indians off until after dark. When he finally rode into camp, he discovered that Weir had not come in, and reported that he was probably killed. The battalion of the 5th Cavalry was turned out at once, and we had an all-night march ahead of us. Just at dawn we reached the place where Weir left Hall, and we took his trail and followed it up until we found his dead body lying cold and stiff on the mountainside. This seemed indeed an unnecessary sacrifice. We returned to the camp as sad a funeral procession as one could imagine.

AN INCIDENT OF THE MARCH

THE MEXICAN ARMY

Thomas A. Janvier

BREAKING THE CHAINS

Military traditions are strong in Mexico. The race that inhabited the Plateau at the time of the Spanish conquest was a fighting race. Each of the several powerful tribes into which it was divided was stirred by a lively desire to fight one or more of the others, and at short intervals this desire was abundantly gratified. The fighting instinct was manifested to a better purpose in the gallant war made against Spain between the years 1810 and 1821, that resulted in Mexican independence; and it was further manifested, together with something akin to the ancient division of the people into rival tribes, in the civil wars which went on almost without cessation for more than half a century after independence was achieved.

It is unfair, however, to blame the Mexicans because they have worked out their salvation slowly. For three centuries they were most grievously priestridden. Three score years of political fermentation was not an unduly long time in which to clear away three hundred years of political impurities.

A REGIMENTAL SCOUT

CAVALRY OF THE LINE

In addition to the sabre, the cavalrymen are armed with Remington carbines (cal. 50). Their horses, excepting the handsome mounts of the officers, are small animals of native breed, as tough and wiry as the men who ride them, and as capable of enduring enormous marches on a scant supply of water and food.

INFANTRY OF THE LINE

The rank and file of the army for the most part is drawn from the lowest classes. For many years the highly objectionable custom has prevailed of drafting into the service various sorts of criminals, and the strong effort that President Diaz is making to put an end to a custom so demoralizing is one of the most commendable of his Army reforms. The practical effect of making the army more or less of a penal institution is to keep good men out of it, while the convict soldiers are prompt to desert whenever occasion offers, and by their example to make desertions frequent.

Sometimes a rather humorous ingenuity is shown in slipping out of the military bondage. In Monterey, one rainy night in March, 1883, more than a score of men belonging to a regiment drawn up at the railway station, in waiting for the arrival of the President, succeeded in getting away by the device of placing their caps on the butts of their muskets, bayonet down, in the ground in their places in the ranks. By the uncertain torchlight the platoons seemed unbroken, and it was only when the order to march was given, and the regiment moved away and left the cap-bearing muskets standing over the ground, that the officers perceived the trick which had been played upon them.

CAVALRY OF THE LINE   INFANTRY OF THE LINE

LOOKING FOR DESERTERS

Recapturing a deserter is anything but an easy matter, for the common people invariably assist him to escape, giving him refuge in hiding and most generously lying about his whereabouts, and his own comrades are not especially zealous in their efforts to recapture him. The burden of the chase usually rests upon the officer in command of the detail, and he frequently has experiences of a sort much more exciting than pleasing. I knew a young lieutenant, but recently graduated from Chapultepec, and all unused to military ways, who was so mauled and tumbled by the big wife of the deserter for whom he was searching that but for the laughing interference in his behalf of his own men he very well might have been shaken to death by her. He came back to barracks with a badly scratched face, some rather serious bruises, and his uniform in a shocking condition; and what was still worse, he came back without the deserter.

TELÉSFORO

On another occasion I had a more closely personal experience of this phase of army life in Mexico. I had hired a lad of twenty or thereabouts as man-of-all-work. Telésforo was a pleasant, good-natured boy, and willing to a degree. But we soon found an exception to his willingness in his strong objection to being sent out of the house. To our surprise, each time that we wanted to send him into the streets he developed suddenly a pain in his inside, from which he recovered with astonishing rapidity when one of the other servants had been sent in his place. He had an anxious manner, and a habit of instantly absenting himself when anybody knocked at the door. Our surprise did not last for a great while, for on the morning of the second day that Telésforo was in our employ I was summoned to an interview with a polite young lieutenant, who courteously apologized for being compelled to disarrange our domestic affairs by taking our servant back to the barrack where he belonged. And away Telésforo went, a pitiably forlorn object, guarded by four grinning soldiers with bared bayonets, and with the polite lieutenant — very much pleased with himself for having effected the capture — jauntily bringing up the rear.

LOOKING FOR DESERTERS

A GENDARME

MEXICAN INFANTRY ON THE MARCH

By far the greater number of enlisted men are of the primitive Mexican stock, whose good-natured brown faces show their freedom from mixture with the race of their Spanish conquerors. They are of the same stock as the men who fought under Cortéz, who helped Nuño de Guzman to conquer Pánuco, Jalisco, and Michoacan, and who served with Alvarado in his campaign in Guatemala. And they have the same soldierly qualities of obedience and bravery now that their ancestors had then. They are capital fighters, especially in short sharp work that can be carried through with a rush and a hurrah. In their many strenuous battles with the French they gained a steadiness, a coolness under fire, and a resoluteness in defeat as well as in victory which has added vastly to the effectiveness of the Mexican troops as a warlike force. As to their capacity for forced marches, and their wiry strength on short supplies of food and water, they are not surpassed by any troops in the world, and in endurance of this sort they are very far superior to the soldiers of North America and Europe.

MEXICAN INFANTRY ON THE MARCH

ON DRESS PARADE

Doubtless the practical impossibility of keeping up any show of smartness in brown linen blouse and trousers — which, with leather sandals (the best foot-gear ever devised for marching), constitutes the undress uniform — has much to do with the general carelessness that apparently is suffered to go unrebuked.

But on dress parade these same easygoing soldiers present a very creditable appearance. Indeed, I never saw anywhere a more soldierly body of men than the force that marched in review past the President on the 5th of May, 1885.

The linen uniforms were replaced by handsome suits of blue cloth, and the sandals by leather shoes; the accouterments and arms were in fine form; and the men, massed in broad columns, bore themselves in as soldierly a fashion as the most rigid disciplinarian could desire. The marching pace of the infantry was almost a double-quick; the cavalry frequently moved at a trot; and some of the batteries dashed by at a gallop.

LIEUTENANT, ENGINEER BATTALION

FULL-DRESS ENGINEER

BUGLER OF CAVALRY

SOLDIER'S PAY

Since the soldier must carry his belongings on his own back or the back of a horse, and since both of these are already sufficiently burdened, the temptation to the common soldier to increase his kit is not strong; and even should he be disposed to provide himself with additional comforts, the limits of his pay would be reached before he had greatly enlarged his outfit. The nominal pay of enlisted men in the infantry is four reales (about thirty-six cents) a day, but they actually receive only two and a half reales, the remainder being reserved in the battalion fund until the termination of their enlistment. Enlisted men in the cavalry and artillery nominally receive five reales, and actually receive three and a half.

YAQUI INDIAN REFUGEES WITH CAPTIVE MEXICAN SOLDIER

THE RURALES

A very important subdivision of the army is the gendarmeria, a force charged with certain classes of police duties, of which the most respectable is that of keeping the highways clear of robbers. The section especially employed as a road guard is known as the Rurales, and is by all odds the most picturesque, and in some respects the most meritorious, body of troops in the Mexican service.

Each man provides his own horse and equipment (excepting his arms), and is paid ten reales a day, out of which he provides rations for himself and forage for his horse. The horses are by far the finest, excepting officers' mounts, in the service, and are so affectionately cared for that they seldom get out of condition, while on review they positively shine. The men are magnificent fellows, fully looking the dare-devils that they actually are.

A RURAL

CHARTERING A NATION

Julian Ralph

CHIEF CROWFOOT

How it came about that we chartered the Blackfoot nation for two days had better not be told in straightforward fashion. There is more that is interesting in going around about the subject, just as in reality we did go around and about the neighborhood of the Indians before we determined to visit them.

The most interesting Indian I ever saw was the late Chief Crowfoot, of the Blackfoot people. When Crowfoot talked, he made laws. While he spoke, his nation listened in silence. He had killed as many men as any Indian warrior alive; he was a mighty buffalo-slayer; he was torn, scarred, and mangled in skin, limb, and bone. He never would learn English or pretend to discard his religion. He was an Indian after the pattern of his ancestors. At eighty-odd years of age there lived no red man who dared answer him back when he spoke his mind. But he was a shrewd man and an archdiplomatist. Because he had no quarrel with the whites, and because a grand old priest was his truest friend, he gave orders that his body should be buried in a coffin, Christian fashion, and as I rode over the plains in the summer of 1890 I saw his burial-place on top of a high hill, and knew that his bones were guarded night and day by watchers from among his people.

"THRUST HIS LANCE THROUGH HIS BODY AND RODE HIM DOWN"

OLD SUN'S WIFE

Old Sun's wife sits in the council of her nation—the only woman, white, red, or black, of whom I have ever heard who enjoys such a prerogative on this continent. She earned her peculiar privileges, if any one ever earned anything.

On the night before the day of her adventure a band of Crows stole a number of horses from a camp of the Gros Ventres, and very artfully trailed their plunder close to the Piegan camp before they turned and made their way to their own lodges. When the Gros Ventres discovered their loss, and followed the trail that seemed to lead to the Piegan camp, the girl and her father, an aged chief, were at a distance from their tepees, unarmed and unsuspecting. Down swooped the Gros Ventres. They killed and scalped the old man, and then their chief swung the young girl upon his horse behind him, and binding her to him with thongs of buckskin, dashed off triumphantly to his own village.

When she and her captor were in sight of the Gros Ventre village, she reached forward and stole the chief's scalping-knife from out of its sheath at his side. With it, still wet with her father's blood, she cut him in the back through the heart. She then freed his body from hers, and tossed him from the horse's back. Leaping to the ground beside his body, she not only scalped him, but cut off his right arm and picked up his gun, and rode madly back to her people, bringing safely with her the three greatest trophies a warrior can wrest from a vanquished enemy. From that day she has boasted the right to wear three eagle feathers.

She was later admitted to the Blackfoot council without a protest, and has since proven that her valor was not sporadic, for she has taken the warpath upon occasion, and other scalps have gone to her credit.

THE ROMANTIC ADVENTURE OF OLD SUN'S WIFE

THE BUFFALO DANCE

And then came the grand spectacle. The vast plain was forgotten, and the great campus within the circle of tents was transformed into a theater. All the tribal heirlooms were in the display, the cherished gewgaws, trinkets, arms, apparel, and finery they had saved from the fate of which they will not admit they are themselves the victims. The traditional Indian with the eagle plumes from crown to heels was there; so was he with the buffalo horns growing out of his skull; so were the idyllic braves in yellow buckskin fringed at every point.

THE BUFFALO DANCE

THE SOLDIER CLAN DANCE

The four braves beat the drum and chanted, until presently a young warrior, hideous with war paint, came out of a tepee and began the dancing. In the course of a few circles around the tomtom he began shouting of valorous deeds he had never performed, for he was too young to have ridden after buffalo or into battle. Presently he pretended to see upon the ground something at once fascinating and awesome. It was the trail of the enemy. Then he danced furiously and more limberly, tossing his head back, shaking his hatchet and his many-tailed shield high aloft, and yelling that he was following the foe, and would not rest while a skull and a scalp-lock remained in conjunction among them. He was joined by three others, and all danced and yelled like madmen. At last the leader came to a sort of standard made of a stick and some cloth, tore it out from where it had been thrust in the ground, and holding it far above his head, pranced once about the circle, and thus ended the dance.

SKETCH IN THE SOLDIER CLAN DANCE

THE PONY WAR DANCE

There were threescore young men in the brilliant equestrian cavalcade. They rode horses that were as wild as themselves. Their evolutions were rude, but magnificent. Now they dashed past us in single file, and next they came helter-skelter, like cattle stampeding. For a while they rode around and around, as on a race-course, but at times they deserted the enclosure, parted into small bands, and were hidden behind the curtains of their own dust, presently to reappear with a mad rush, yelling like maniacs, and brandishing their arms and their finery wildly on high.

For ninety minutes we watched the glorious riding, the splendid horses, the brilliant trappings, and the paroxysmal fervor of the excited Indians. The earth trembled beneath the dashing of the riders; the air palpitated with the noise of their war cries and bells.

We had enjoyed a never-to-be-forgotten privilege. It was as if we had seen the ghosts of a dead people ride back to re-enact scenes in an era that had vanished. It was as if the sudden up-flashing of a smoldering fire lighted, once again and for an instant, the scene it had ceased to illumine.

A FANTASY FROM THE PONY WAR DANCE

TEXAN TYPES AND CONTRASTS

Lee C. Harby

THE TWO CULTURES

In the many quaint and artistic phases of life which Texas presents there are none more alluring than those in which the Spanish peoples play the principal part. Wherever found, these Texo-Mexicans are picturesque, and their admixture with the population renders the State fertile in vivid contrast and rich local coloring. Even in the large cities, where they are in such small proportion, these people are distinctly noticeable from the comparisons they afford. Only in the cities of Texas can be found that peculiar fusion of American civilization with Mexican life.

A VAQUERO

SCENES AT THE SATURDAY MARKET

Pursuing the odd, the new, and the characteristic takes the tourist to the Saturday evening market held at Houston. The people who congregate here make it a remarkable scene, for the vendors alone represent every race and nationality.

The Negro market gardener raises all that he offers, from the fat turkeys, ready-dressed or alive in coops, to the tiny bird-peppers, brilliant in hue, small as a pea, hot as fire, and delightful in flavor, which grow wild along the bayou that borders his land.

Nearby on the sidewalk a Chinese peddler displays his wares. He has his pigtail neatly pinned up, and his blouse and shoes are models of cleanliness. "Anytling a day?" he asks, exhibiting wonderful fans and cushions, brushes, tea-pots, Chinese lilies, and what not.

Here is a little German woman, face sharp and puckered into innumerable wrinkles; but her balls of hand-cheese, strewed with caraway seeds, are white and appetizing. She has some put away in a can, which she tells you "shmeck gut" but when uncovered they are as yellow as gold, and smell to heaven; yet these her German customers prefer.

A thin-faced Italian has a wagon laden with game, all killed close by: rabbits and squirrels, bunches of partridges, braces of prairie-chicken, and dozens of snipe tied together by the neck, some wild geese, ducks of all kinds, and a single sandhill crane.

Within the building stretches a row of vegetable stalls, all tended by women, German and Irish exclusively, clean dressed and hatless. Their wares make a pretty show: no hot-bed products are here, no garden truck from other states, but all home-raised.

MEXICAN VENDOR AND CHILD

OX CART, TRAIGUEN

JUAN AND JUANITA

The Rio Grande is the land of romance and of poetry, of legend, of warrior, and of priest, for from here stretching back to the Nueces lies the home of the Spanish element of the population. Here, in a clearing of the thick chaparral which borders the white winding road, stands an adobe house. The shadows of night fall thick about it, and soon from within its master comes, leaving its door wide open as he mounts his mustang and rides away to the nearest village, a mile or more distant. The warm red light of the mesquite fire fills up the portal, and presently into this radiance passes a woman — young, slim, and handsome, with the languor and passion of the South within the depth of her dark Spanish eyes. For a moment she stands and peers out, as if to pierce through the night, her form outlined against the glowing background; then drawing her rebozo about her half-bare bosom, she turns, and taking a guitar, sings in sweet high tones a little Spanish song.

The song is evidently a signal; scarcely have its notes died away before a tall, lithe young Mexican creeps out from the thickest part of the chaparral and makes his way into the house. He knows the danger, or fears treachery perhaps, for as their lips meet and the door closes behind them, the light flashes and plays on the long, keen blade of a knife he holds unsheathed in his hand.

JUAN AND JUANITA

THE TORTILLA MAKER

Every yard almost has an oven, built out of earth and rock, half under and half over the ground; here they bake their meats and some kinds of cakes, but their own bread is tortillas. These are made by an interesting and peculiar process. The Indian-corn is boiled whole in water, into which a little unslaked lime is thrown, until the grain is tender. It is then taken out, washed, put into clear cold water, and allowed to soak all night. In the morning it is drained dry and crushed into flour between two stones — the bottom one like a three-cornered tray on legs of uneven height, so that it slopes downward; the upper, like a rolling-pin. They place the tray upon the floor, and kneeling, they mash and roll the grain until it becomes a beautiful, white, starchy flour. That is mixed with water into a paste, next kneaded and flattened out between the hands into broad, very thin cakes. In the meantime the mesquite fire in the corner of the jacal has burned into a grand bed of coals; on this is thrown a flat sheet of iron, which is soon hot. Here the cakes are placed, and brown instantaneously; they are turned, and in a minute ready to be eaten. They are good, too, but need salt, for the Mexican mixes none in his bread.

THE TORTILLA MAKER

A MEXICAN DUEL

The manners of the Mexican have a grave decorum that is worthy of imitation, and they are wonderfully law-abiding, as far as riots or quarrels are concerned; but make no Mexican your enemy, or else avoid the darkness of night and of shadow, should he be within reach. He will smile in your face as you pass, then wheel and sheathe his knife in your back. Their warfare is not open, and hence has none of the frank, lusty, rollicking bravado of the cowboy, who gives a man a chance always in his quarrels, and would as soon be shot at as shoot.

A MEXICAN DUEL

A MEXICAN BUCCARO

On these vast grazing-grounds of the West, the cowboy has his home. He is ever a picturesque figure, whether in groups or dismounted and standing alone on the great prairie, watching the train flash past him, broad-hatted and clad in buckskin pants, with many little fringes down the seams. His flannel shirt and short jacket look well on him, and his Winchester and lariat are slung from the pommel of his saddle. His horse stands as still as a statue, untied and patient, with drooping head, awaiting his master's will. He knows every tone of his voice, and is trained to obey every word; he is tough and wiry and not easily tired, coming of the old mustang stock, which sprang from the steeds of Cortéz's men.

A MEXICAN BUCCARO

THE NEW LIFE

Cowboy life has in the past few years lost much of its roughness. The cattle barons have discharged most of the men who drank, and have frowned so persistently upon gambling that little of it is done. Cards and whiskey being put away, there is small temptation for disorderly conduct; so it is only when they reach some large city, and not on duty, that they indulge in a genuine spree. On the ranches kept under fence they have little to do when not on the drive or in branding-time, the cattle being all safely enclosed. But they must take their turns at line riding, which means a close inspection of the fences, and the repair of all breaks and damages.

It is not a life of hardship, and pays well enough. Everything is furnished to them free and of the very best, and in addition they are paid thirty dollars per month. Each party stays out from two to three weeks at a time; but they take with them the finest of camp wagons, with beds and cooking utensils, the best of groceries of all kinds, and as excellent a cook as money can employ. The prairies are full of game, and their rifles are ever handy. The life is free, fascinating, and peculiarly healthy.

A MEXICAN HORSE-TRADER

A SAMPLE STEED

"THE APACHES ARE COMING"

Away off on the frontier are still found, here and there, specimens of those strong, brave early settlers who literally live with their lives in their hands, establishing themselves far beyond the outposts of civilization, not knowing at what time the red men might raid upon them and lay their homes in ashes. Sturdy houses those, stockades they might better be called, houses that are forts as well as homes. And there is found a rare hospitality which asks no questions, but entertains the wayfarer, giving him all that he requires "without money and without price."

"THE APACHES ARE COMING"

ON THE INDIAN RESERVATIONS

Frederic Remington

DISTRIBUTION OF BEEF AT THE SAN CARLOS AGENCY

The San Carlos reservation is a vast tract of desert and mountain, and near the center of it, on the Gila River, is a great flat plain where the long, low adobe buildings of the agency are built. The San Carlos is a hotter place than I ever intend to visit again. A man who is used to breathing the fresh air of New York Bay is in no condition to enjoy at one and the same time a dinner and the Turkish bath that accompanies it.

From the parade in front of our tent I could see the long lines of horses, mules, and burros trooping into the agency from all quarters. Ordinarily the Indians are scattered for forty miles in every direction; but this was ration-day, and they were all together. Hundreds of ponies, caparisoned in all sorts of fantastic ways, were standing around. Young girls of the San Carlos tribe flitted about, attracting my attention by the queer ornaments which, in token of their virginity, they wear in their hair. Tall Yuma bucks galloped past with their long hair flying out behind. The squaws crowded around the exit and received the great chunks of beef which a native butcher threw to them.

DISTRIBUTION OF BEEF AT THE SAN CARLOS AGENCY

THE GAMBLERS

These Territory Apaches are very different from their brothers of the mountains. They are good-looking, but are regarded contemptuously by other Indians and also by the traders. I spent an evening in one of their tepees watching a game of monte, and the gambling passion was developed almost to insanity. They sat and glared at the cards, their dark faces gleaming with avarice, cunning, and excitement.

"BIG SUNDAYS"

The Fourth of July and Christmas are the "white man's big Sundays" to the Indians, and they always expect the regular horse-race appropriations. The cavalrymen contribute purses and the Indians run their ponies. Extra beeves are killed, and the red men have always a great regard for the "big Sundays."

As we approach the agency it is the hour for the race, and the throng moves to some level plain nearby, where a large ring is formed by the Indians on horseback.

An elderly Indian of great dignity of presence steps into the ring, and with a graceful movement throws his long red blanket to the ground and drops on his knees before it to receive the wagers of such that desire to make them. Men walk up and throw in silver dollars and every sort of personal property imaginable. A Winchester rifle and a large nickel-plated Colt's revolver are laid on the grass near me by a cowboy and an Indian, and then each goes away. It was a wager, and I thought they might well have confidence in their stakeholder — mother earth.

INDIAN TERRITORY APACHES PLAYING MONTE   IN THE BETTING-RING

THE FOURTH OF JULY RACE

It was to be a flying start, and they jockeyed a good deal and could not seem to get off. But presently a puff of smoke came from the rifle held aloft by the Kiowa starter, and his horse reared. The report reached us, and with a scurry the five ponies came away from the scratch, followed by a cloud of dust. The quirts flew through the air at every jump. The ponies bunched and pattered away at a nameless rate, for the quarter-race pony is quick of stride. Nearer and nearer they came, the riders lying low on their horses' necks, whipping and ki-yi-yi-ing. The dust in their wake swept backward and upward, and with a rush they came over the scratch, with the roan pony ahead and my little Mexican fellow holding his quirt aloft, and his little eyes snapping with the nervous excitement of the great event. He had beaten the invincible bay stallion, the pride of this Comanche tribe, and as he rode back to his father his face had the settled calm which nothing could penetrate, and which befitted his dignity as a young runner.

INDIAN HORSE-RACE—COMING OVER THE SCRATCH

TALKING MUSQUASH

Julian Ralph

TALKING MUSQUASH

The most sensational bit of "musquash talk" in more than a quarter of a century among the Hudson Bay employees was started the other day, when Sir Donald A. Smith, the president of the oldest of England's great trading companies, sent a type-written letter to Winnipeg. The reader may imagine for himself what a wrench civilization would have gotten if the world had laid down its goosequills and taken up the typewriter all in the same day. And that is precisely what Sir Donald Smith had done. Talking business in the fur trade has always been called "talking musquash (musk-rat)," and after that letter came, the turn taken by that sort of talk suggested a general fear that from the Arctic to Queen Charlotte's Islands the canvassers for competing machines would be racing to all the posts, each to prove that his instrument can pound out more words in a minute than any other.

In these isolated posts, life has always been taken very gently. One day, when a factor had heard that the battle of Waterloo had been fought and won by the English, he deliberately loaded the best trade gun in the storehouse and went out and fired it into the pulseless woods, although it was two years after the battle, and the disquieted Old World had long known the greater news that Napoleon was caged in St. Helena. Today, the only reassuring note in the "musquash talk" is sounded when the subject of candles is reached, for the Governor and committee in London still pursue their deliberations by candlelight.

Rebellion against their fate is idle. The truth is that the trickle of immigration which their ancient monopoly first brought into that land is now sweeping over their vast territory, and altering more than its face. A great many factors now find villages around their old forts, and railroads close at hand, and Law setting up its officers at their doors, so that in a great part of the territory the romance of the old life, and their authority as well, has fled.

TALKING MUSQUASH

THE ARCTIC BARRENS

There is a wide belt called the Arctic Barrens all along the north, but below that, at some distance west of Hudson Bay, the great forests of Canada bridge across the region north of the prairie and the plains, and cross the Rocky Mountains to reach the Pacific. In the far north the musk-ox descends almost to meet the moose and the deer, and on the near slope of the Rockies the wood-buffalo—larger, darker, and fiercer than the bison of the plains—still roams as far south as where the buffalo ran highest in the days when he existed.

THE PERILS OF WINTER

Through all this northern country the cold in winter registers forty and even fifty degrees below zero, and the travel is by dogs and sleds. There the men in camp may be said to dress to go to bed. They leave their winter's store of dried meat and frozen fish out-of-doors on racks all winter; they hear from civilization twice a year at the utmost; and when supplies have run out at the posts, we have heard of their boiling the parchment sheets they use instead of glass in their windows, and of cooking the fat out of beaver skins to keep from starving, though beaver is so precious that such recourse could only be had when the horses and dogs had been eaten.

BUFFALO MEAT FOR THE POST

INDIAN HUNTER HANGING DEER OUT OF THE REACH OF WOLVES

THE COURRIER DU BOIS AND THE SAVAGE

The old courriers du bois were of Norman and Breton stock, loving a wild, free life, and in complete sympathy with the Indian, took the squaws to wife, learned the Indian dialects, and shared their food and adventures with the tribes. These rough and hardy woodsmen began at an early day to settle near the trading-posts. Sometimes they established what might be called villages, but were really close imitations of Indian camps, composed of a cluster of skin tepees, racks of fish or meat, and a tumult of women, children, and dogs. In each tepee was the fireplace, beneath the flue formed by the open top of the habitation, and around it were the beds of brush, covered with soft hides, the inevitable copper kettle, the babies swaddled in blankets or moss bags, the gun and paddle, and the chunks and strips of raw meat hanging overhead in the smoke.

THE COURRIER DU BOIS AND THE SAVAGE

RESISTING A BRIBE

As more and more entered the wilderness, and at last came to be supported as voyageurs by the competing fur companies, there grew up a class of mixed-bloods who spoke English and French, married Indians, and were as much at home with the Indians as with the whites. But when they became turbulent and murderous — first on the attacks on Selkirk's colony, and next during the Riel rebellion — the Indians remained quiet. They defined their position when, in 1819, they were tempted with great bribes to massacre the Red River colonists. "No," said they, "the colonists are our friends."

RIVAL TRADERS RACING TO THE INDIAN CAMP

THE PLAN THAT FAILED

The men who sought to excite them to murder were the officers of the Northwest Company, who brought furs with them, to be sure, but the colonists had shared with the Indians in poverty and plenty, giving now and taking then. All were alike to the red man — friends, white men, and the race that had taken so many of them to wife. Therefore they went to the colonists to tell them what was being planned against them, and not from that day to this has an Indian band taken the war-path against the Canadians.

A FUR TRADER IN THE COUNCIL TEPEE

THE FACTOR

The factor is still, as he has always been, responsible only to himself for the discipline and management of his post. When one thinks of the lives of these men, hidden away in forest, mountain chain, plain, or arctic barren, seeing the same very few faces year in and year out, with breaches of this monotonous routine only once a year when the winter's furs are brought in, and once a year when the mail-packet arrives, one wonders the reason for choosing that company's service. Yet they will tell you that there is a fascination in it.

Picture a factor on a round of his outposts, or a chief factor racing through a great district. If he is riding, he fancies that princes and lords would envy him could they see his luxurious comfort. Fancy him in a dog-cariole of the best pattern — a little suggestive of a burial-casket, to be sure, in its shape, but gaudily painted, and so full of soft warm furs that the man within is enveloped like a chrysalis in a cocoon.

THE FACTOR'S FANCY TOBOGGAN

THE VOYAGEUR

The French Canadians and mixed-bloods, who were the voyageurs and hunters, made a striking appearance. They used to wear the company's regulation light blue capotes, or coats, in winter, with flannel shirts, either red or blue, and corduroy trousers gartered at the knee with beadwork. They all wore gaudy worsted belts, long heavy woollen stockings with fringed leggins, fancy moccasins, and tuques, or feather-decorated caps bound with tinsel bands. In mild weather their costume was formed of a blue striped cotton shirt, corduroys, blue cloth leggins bound with orange ribbons, the inevitable sash or worsted belt, and moccasins. Every hunter carried a powder-horn slung from his neck, and in his belt a tomahawk, which often served as a pipe.

VOYAGEURS IN CAMP FOR THE NIGHT

"HUSKIE" DOGS ON THE FROZEN HIGHWAY

The dogs and sleds form a very interesting part of the Hudson Bay outfit. One does not need to go very deep into western Canada to meet with them. The dogs are of a peculiar breed, and are called "huskies" — undoubtedly a corruption of the word "Esquimaux." They are often as large as the ordinary Newfoundland dog, but their legs are shorter, and even more hairy, and the hair along their necks, from their shoulders to their skulls, stands erect in a thick bristling mass. They have the long snouts, sharp-pointed ears, and the tails of wolves, and their cry is a yelp rather than a bark. Like wolves they are apt to yelp in chorus at sunrise and at sunset. They are disciplined only when at work, and then are so surprisingly obedient, tractable, and industrious as to plainly show that though their nature is savage and wolfish, they could be reclaimed by domestication. As it is, in their packs, their battles among themselves are terrible, and they are dangerous when loose.

A typical dog-sled is very like a toboggan. It is formed of two thin pieces of oak or birch lashed together with buckskin thongs and turned up high in front. It is usually about nine feet in length by sixteen inches wide. A leather cord is run along the outer edges for fastening whatever may be put upon the sled. Varying numbers of dogs are harnessed to such sleds, but the usual number is four. The leader, or foregoer, is always the best of the team. The dog next to him is called the steady dog, and the last is named the steer dog. As a rule, these faithful animals are treated harshly, if not brutally. It is a Hudson Bay axiom that no man who cannot curse in three languages is fit to drive them.

"HUSKIE" DOGS ON THE FROZEN HIGHWAY

MODERN TIMES

Today the service is very little more inviting than in the olden time. The loneliness and removal from the touch of civilization remain throughout a vast region; the arduous journeys by sled and canoe remain; the dangers of flood and frost are undiminished. Of all the former charm of Indian costuming one sees now only a trace here and there in a few tribes, while in many only the moccasin and tepee remain. Most of the descendants of the old-time voyageur preserve only his worsted belt, his knife, and his cap and his moccasins at most. Now, the steamboat has been pressed into service, and reliance on the more traditional modes of transportation is passing. But in return the horrors of intertribal war and the uncertainties of a precarious foothold among the fierce and turbulent bands have nearly vanished; but there was a spice in them that added to the fascination of the service.

IN A STIFF CURRENT

CANADA'S EL DORADO

Julian Ralph

ON THE WESTERN COAST OF CANADA

British Columbia is of immense size, yet it has been all but overlooked by man, and may be said to be an empire with only one wagon road, and that is but a blind artery halting in the middle of the country.

One gets the idea of the swarms of fish that infest those waters by the knowledge that before nets were used the herring and the colachan, or candle-fish, were swept into their large boats by an implement formed by studding a ten-foot pole with spikes or nails. This was swept among the fish in the water, and the boats were speedily filled with the creatures that were impaled upon the spikes. Once they sold the fish to the Hudson's Bay Company, and ate what surplus they did not sell. Now they work in the canneries or fish for them in summer, and hunt, trap, or loaf the rest of the time.

SALMON

The main salmon rivers are the Fraser, Skeena, and Nasse rivers, but the fish also swarm in the inlets into which smaller streams empty. Setting aside the stories of water so thick with salmon that a man might walk upon their backs, as well as that tale of the stagecoach that was upset by salmon banking themselves against it when it was crossing a fording-place, there still exist absolutely trustworthy accounts of swarms which at their height cause the largest rivers to seem alive with these fish. In such cases the ripple of their back fins frets the entire surface of the stream. I have seen photographs that show the fish in incredible numbers, side by side, like logs in a raft, and I have the word of a responsible man for the statement that he has gotten all the salmon needed for a small camp, day after day, by walking to the edge of a river and jerking the fish out with a common poker.

THE SALMON CACHE

INDIAN SALMON FISHING ON THE THRASHER

MAKING THE BIG CANOE

The coast Indians are splendid sailors, and their dugouts do not always come off second best in racing with the boats of the white men. With a primitive yet ingeniously made tool, like an adze, these natives laboriously pick out the heart of a great cedar log, and shape its outer sides into the form of a boat. When the log is properly hollowed, they fill it with water, and then drop in stones which they have heated in a fire. Thus they steam the boat so that they may spread the sides and fit in the crossbars which keep it strong and preserve its shape. These dugouts are sometimes sixty feet long, and are used for whaling and long voyages on rough seas. They are capable of carrying tons of the salmon or colachan or herring, of which these people, who live as their fathers did, catch sufficient for their maintenance throughout a whole year.

After a dugout is hollowed and steamed, a prow and stern are added of separate wood. The prow is always a work of art, and greatly beautifies the boat. It is in form like the breast, neck, and bill of a bird, but the head is intended to represent that of a savage animal, and is so painted. A mouth is cut into it, ears are carved on it, and eyes are painted on the sides; bands of gay paint are put upon the neck, and the whole exterior of the boat is then painted red or black, with an ornamental line of another color along the edge or gunwale.

GOING TO THE POTLATCH—BIG CANOE, NORTHWEST COAST

THE POTLATCH

In the original settlements in that territory a peculiar institution occasioned gala times for the Indians now and then. This was the potlatch, a thing to us so foreign that we have no word or phrase to give it meaning. It is a feast or merrymaking at the expense of some man who has earned or saved what he deems considerable wealth, and who desires to distribute every iota of it at once in edibles and drinkables among the people of his tribe or village. He does this because he aspires to a chieftainship, or merely for the credit of a potlatch — a high distinction. Indians have been known to throw away such a sum of money that their potlatch has been given in a huge shed built for the feast, that hundreds have been fed and made drunk, and that blankets and ornaments have been distributed in addition to the feast.

The custom has a new significance now. It is the white man who is to enjoy a greater than all previous potlatches in that region. The treasure has been garnered during the ages by time and nature, and the province itself is offered as the feast.

THE POTLATCH

ARTIST WANDERINGS AMONG THE CHEYENNES

Frederic Remington

THE SIGN LANGUAGE

A dark-skinned old Arapaho rode up, and our Caddo guide saluted him. They began to converse in the sign language as they sat on their ponies, and we watched them with great interest. With graceful gestures they made the signs and seemed immediately and fully to comprehend each other. As the old Arapaho's face cut dark against the sunset, I thought it the finest Indian profile I had ever seen. He was arrayed in the full Indian costume of these latter days, with leggings, beaded moccasins, and a sheet wrapped around his waist and thighs. The Caddo, on the contrary, was a progressive man. His hair was cropped in Cossack style; he wore a hat, boots, and a great "slicker," or cowboy's oilskin coat. For the space of half an hour they thus interested each other. We speculated on the meaning of the signs, and could often follow them, but they abbreviated so much and did it all so fast that we missed the full meanings of their conversation.

A CHEYENNE CAMP

A great level prairie of waving green was dotted with the brown toned white canvas lodges, and standing near them were brush "ramadas," or sheds, and also wagons. In little groups all over the plain were scattered pony herds, and about the camp could be seen forms wearing bright blankets or wrapped in ghostlike cotton sheets. Little columns of blue smoke rose here and there, and gathered in front of one lodge was squatted a group of men. A young squaw dressed in a bright calico gown stood near a ramada and bandied words with the interpreter while I sketched. Presently she was informed that I had made her picture, and she ran off, laughing at what she considered an unbecoming trick on the part of her entertainer.

THE SIGN LANGUAGE

A CHEYENNE CAMP

THE AGENCY AT FORT SILL

The Cheyenne agency buildings are situated about a mile and a half from Fort Sill. The great brick building is imposing. A group of stores and little white dwelling-houses surround it, giving it much the effect of a New England village. Wagons, saddled ponies, and Indians are generally disposed about the vicinity and give life to the scene.

Fifteen native policemen in the employ of the agency do the work and take care of the place. They are uniformed in cadet grey, and with their beaded white moccasins and their revolvers are neat and soldierly looking.

AN AGENCY POLICEMAN

THE BRANDING CHUTE AT THE BEEF ISSUE

The agent came to the corral and together with the army officer inspected the cattle to be given out. With loud cries the cowboys in the corral forced the steers into the chute, and crowding and clashing they came through into the scales. The gate of the scales was opened and a half-dozen frightened steers crowded down the chute and packed themselves in an unyielding mass at the other end. A tall Arapaho policeman seized a branding-iron, and mounting the platform of the chute poised his iron and with a quick motion forced it on the back of the living beast. With a wild but useless plunge and a loud bellow of pain the steer shrunk from the hot contact, but it was all over, and a long black "I.D." disfigured the surface of the skin. This was done so that any Indian having subsequently a hide in his possession would be enabled to satisfy roving cattle inspectors that they were not to be suspected of killing stock.

THE BRANDING CHUTE AT THE BEEF ISSUE

THE BEEF ISSUE

Opposite the branding-chute were drawn up thirty young bucks on their ponies, with their rifles and revolvers in hand. The agent shouted the Indian names from the book, and a very engaging lot of cognomens they were. A policeman on the platform designated a particular steer which was to be the property of each man as his name was called. After all the steers had been marked, the terrified brutes found the gate at the end of the chute suddenly opened by the police guard. The gates flew wide, and the maddened brutes poured forth, charging swiftly away in a wild impulse to escape the vicinity of the crowd of humanity. The young bucks in the group broke away, and each one, singling out his steer, followed at top speed, with rifle or six-shooter in hand. I desired to see the whole proceeding, and mounting my cavalry horse followed two young bucks who seemed to have a steer possessed of unusual speed.

The lieutenant had previously told me that the shooting at the steers was often wild and reckless, and advised me to look sharp or I might have to "pack a bullet." Puffs of smoke and the "pop! pop!" of the guns came from all over the plain. Now a steer would drop, stricken by some lucky shot. It was buffalo-hunting all over again, and was evidently greatly enjoyed by the young men.

Peace and contentment reign while the beef holds out, which is not long, as the ration is insufficient. This is purposely so, as it is expected that the Indians will seek to increase a scant food supply by raising corn. It does not have that effect, however. By selling ponies, which they have in great numbers, they manage to get money; but the financial future of the Cheyennes is not flattering.

STEER-HUNTING

THE GREAT PLAINS OF CANADA

C. A. Kenaston

THE PLAINS IN WINTER

No words or pictures can adequately convey the real impressions which these regions make upon one who travels over them in long journeys in summer and winter. It is one thing to talk of vastness and solitude and silence, of transparent air and illimitable sunshine in summer, or of fierce, howling winter tempests shutting down about the lonely traveler as he struggles forward with no friendly shrub or tree or sheltering hill greeting his tired senses. But it is quite another thing to have experienced it at first-hand.

CANADIAN MOUNTED POLICE ON A WINTER EXPEDITION

A HALF-BREED SETTLEMENT

From the aspen the half-breed and the Hudson's Bay hunter or trapper build their rude cabins, the logs rarely exceeding eight or ten inches in diameter. These houses are generally small, perhaps sixteen to eighteen feet square, and rarely more than six feet high at the corners. Each consists of a single room, which serves for all the purposes of family life, having one low, battened door turning on wooden hinges. It is roofed with alternate layers of prairie-grass and mud to the thickness of half a foot or more, resting on a layer of poplar poles placed close together. A single small window, generally unglazed, serves the usual purposes of such an opening. The floor is of puncheons of the same wood as the rest of the house, or is simply the clay tramped hard and smooth. The chimney and fireplace are made of mud molded upon a rude structure of sticks to give it form and stability. Thus after a few days work, with an axe as his only implement, he constructs a house which makes up for all its deficiencies by its inexpensiveness and its comfort in a hyperborean climate.

PONIES HERDING AROUND SMUDGE FIRES

During July and August mosquitos do abound, and they are attended by coadjutors of no mean powers — sand-flies, black-flies, deer-flies, and I know not how many others, who conspire to make life for man and animal nothing less than a burden. So numerous and virulent are they that animals grow thin in flesh during the period of their existence, and on the Athabasca River horses and cattle perish outright from their attacks. At night the traveler's animals are often stampeded by them, and the usual precaution is to make a dense, dank fire of green boughs and sods, and in this acrid smoke a passable degree of comfort can be had. From such a smoke it would be impossible to stampede a band of horses, and for the choicest positions in it they will fight with teeth and hoofs.

A HALF-BREED SETTLEMENT

PONIES HERDING AROUND SMUDGE FIRES

BUFFALO TRACKS

But the most impressive signs of the abundance of nobler animal life in recent times are the countless buffalo-trails found almost everywhere. Like the cart-trails they are worn deep into the soil, and they remain unchanged for years. While feeding or resting, the buffalo are scattered about, and they make no permanent impression of their presence; but when they are going to water or are traveling to new pastures, they move in single file behind the leader of the herd, and a trail is speedily formed by their sharp hoofs. On their now-deserted pasturing-grounds these trails cut the surface in every direction, now and then marked by the wallowing-places worn deep in the ground, where each animal followed the leader not only in marching, but in taking a dry wash for health and comfort. Up-hill and down-hill these paths wind and wind. Even on the edges of the hogbacks in the valley of the Red Deer River, and on the almost vertical faces, where no horse can find a footing, and a man would find difficulty in going, the buffalo found an easy road for his sure-footed majesty.

THE RETURN FROM THE FALL BUFFALO-HUNT

THE HARSH LAND

Until the farmer came to look upon these broad acres as furnishing land for cultivation of crops and for the raising of cattle, there was little to attract men, civilized or uncivilized, to make their homes here. Nature was forbidding, and offered few natural products for the subsistence of human beings; fuel was scarce and poor, water was of the meanest description, and a climate of the utmost rigor prevailed. The presence of fur-bearing animals in former times, now sadly lessened, alone held out inducement to wandering tribes of Indians, who could clothe themselves from the fruits of the chase and feed their hungry bodies with the carcasses of the slain.

A BLACKFOOT INDIAN

ALL THAT REMAINS

It is not long since the noble buffalo was the monarch of these lonely regions. In favorite localities, where they once fed in countless droves, their bones and horns lie scattered on every hand, bleaching and slowly decomposing in the drying wind. At one time in my wanderings I came, near the Eyebrow Hills, to a tract some hundreds of miles in extent, already scathed by prairie fires and left black and charred. The coal-black surface was thickly dotted with the white bones of the buffalo, which, in some merciless onslaught of the hunters, had fallen there by the thousands for the paltry booty of their hides. Just where they fell, they lay scattered over miles of country, their bones being the only mementos of their happy, crowding, noble animal life. As the skeletons gleamed white in the darkness and the silence of night, the impression made on the thoughtful observer was depressing indeed.

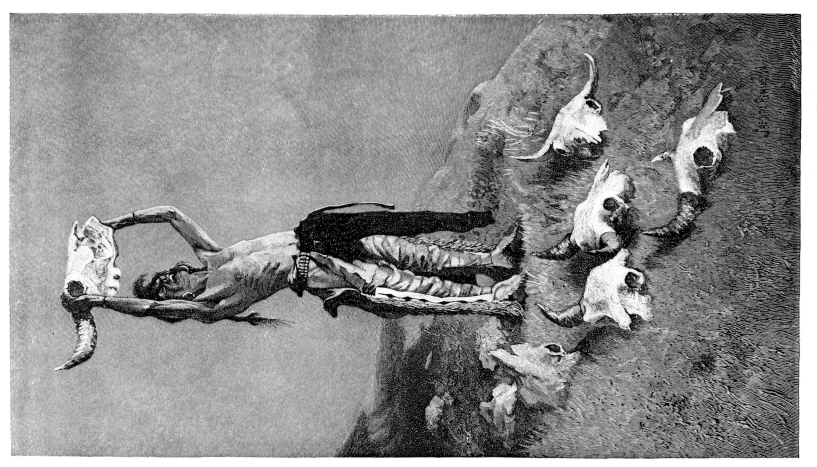

CONJURING BACK THE BUFFALO

BIBLIOGRAPHY

     x. Branding a Horse. *Century*, April 1888

   xiii. Cow-Boys of Arizona: Roused by a Scout. *Harper's Weekly*, December 25, 1882

    xv. The Apache War: Indian Scouts on Geronimo's Trail. *Harper's Weekly*, January 9, 1886

The First Emigrant Train to California. John Bidwell. *Century*, November 1890

    xx. A Recruit from Civilization. *Century*, November 1890

    3. On the Way to the Platte. *Century*, November 1890

    5. Fort Laramie in 1849. *Century*, November 1890

    7. An Emigrant Encampment. *Century*, July 1891

    9. A Peril of the Plains. *Century*, November 1890

   11. Splitting the Herd. *Century*, November 1890

      Thirsty Oxen Stampeding for Water. *Century*, July 1891

   13. Crossing Water to Escape a Prairie Fire. *Century*, November 1890

   15. Water! *Century*, November 1890

   17. Abandoned. *Century*, November 1890

Horses of the Plains. Frederic Remington. *Century*, January 1889

   18. The Indian Pony. *Century*, January 1889

   21. A Texan Pony. *Century*, January 1889

      A "Cayuse." *Century*, January 1889

   23. Broncos and Timber Wolves. *Century*, January 1889

   25. Ponies Pawing in the Snow. *Century*, January 1889

      Horse of the Canadian Northwest. *Century*, January 1889

   27. Spanish Horse of Northern Mexico. *Century*, January 1889

      A Bronco in Central Park. *Century*, January 1889

The Home Ranch. Theodore Roosevelt. *Century*, March 1888

   28. A Montana Type. *Century*, March 1888

   31. In with the Horse Herd. *Century*, March 1888

   33. Roping in a Horse-Corral. *Century*, March 1888

   35. A Deep Ford. *Century*, March 1888

      In a Bog-Hole. *Century*, February 1888

   37. The Midday Meal. *Century*, February 1888

   39. A Bucking Bronco. *Century*, March 1888

      Cruising for Stock. *Century*, March 1888

   41. The Outlying Camp. *Century*, February 1888

      Line Riding in Winter. *Century*, March 1888

   43. Cattle Drifting before the Storm. *Century*, March 1888

   45. Thanksgiving Dinner for the Ranch. *Harper's Weekly*, November 24, 1888

A Scout with the Buffalo Soldiers. Frederic Remington. *Century*, April 1889

   46. A Pull at the Canteen. *Century*, April 1889

   49. Lieutenant Carter P. Johnson. *Harper's Weekly*, December 22, 1888

   51. The Patient Pack-Mule. *Century*, March 1891

      Recreations of a "Mounted Infantryman." *Century*, March 1891

   53. Infantryman in Field Costume. *Century*, March 1891

      Apache Signal Fire. *Century*, March 1891

   55. A Pool in the Desert. *Century*, April 1889

      Marching on the Mountains. *Century*, April 1889

   57. Marching in the Desert. *Century*, April 1889

   59. One of the Real Heroes of Hard Marching. *Harper's Weekly*, December 22, 1888

      A Retiring Scout. *Harper's Weekly*, December 22, 1888

      In the Desert. *Harper's Weekly*, December 22, 1888

      "Laying Back" on the Trail. *Harper's Weekly*, December 22, 1888

   61. A Tumble from the Trail. *Century*, April 1889

Frederic Remington: The American West is an official publication of The American Museum of Natural History, New York, New York. We wish to extend our appreciation to David Ryus and Alan Ternes of the Museum for their assistance.

The original wood engravings were reproduced with kind permission from the collections of the Akron-Summit County Public Library and Kent State University Libraries.

The original illustrations were photographed in fine line by the Graphic Arts Corporation of Ohio, Toledo. The body type has been set in Clarendon Light by Graphic Composition, Inc., Athens, Georgia. Book design by Gary Bielski, Salem, Ohio.

Philip R. St. Clair, EDITOR
Mark J. Stratman, PRODUCTION DIRECTOR
Barry L. Kessel, EDITOR
Murray R. Bowes, PUBLISHER